Tales of Chinatown

By Joe Bruno

Knickerbocker Publishing Company

© 2016, Joe Bruno
(jbruno999@aol.com)

George Appo – "The Most Successful Pickpocket in New York City's History" and the Son of Convicted Murderer - Quimbo Appo

His father was a crazed Chinese killer, and his mother was an Irish alcoholic. As a result of his lack of proper upbringing, George Appo's mission in life was to be the quintessential "good fellow."

George Appo's definition of the phrase "good fellow," was a man who was an expert thief, one who would not cooperate with authorities, and one who would absolutely refuse to testify in court, even against his enemies.

Appo wrote in his 99-page autobiography, which was never published, "What constitutes a 'good fellow' in the eyes and estimation of the underworld is a nervy crook, a money getter and a spender. A 'good fellow' valiantly accepts the consequences and punishment of an arrest, even if the crime was committed by another. A 'good fellow' was a member of a fraternity of thieves."

In the late 1840's, George Appo's father, Quimbo Appo, ran his own tea business in New York City before he moved to New Haven, Connecticut. In 1855, Quimbo Appo met Catherine Fitzpatrick, an Irish immigrant who was in America only for a few years. They married, and in 1856, Catherine Appo gave birth to two children. The first reportedly died in childbirth, but the second was described as, "A handsome, healthy boy, very sprightly, as white as his mother, a Yankee boy to all appearances, with only the Chinaman's breadth between his eyes."

Shortly after George Appo was born, his father returned with his family to New York City. After working as a tea tester for several companies, in 1859 Quimbo Appo opened his own tea store on Third Avenue, between Seventh and Eighth Streets.

Quimbo Appo had a violent temper, worsened by his wife's incessant drunkenness. On March 8, 1859, Quimbo Appo came home from work and found his wife, as usual, three sheets to the wind. He began beating Catherine Appo so viciously, the landlady of their building, Mary Fletcher, and two other tenants, Margaret Butler and Mary Gavigan, interceded and tried to stop the beating. Quimbo Appo became so enraged, he pulled out a knife and stabbed Fletcher twice in the chest. Fletcher fell fatally wounded to the floor, screaming, "My God." Quimbo Appo then stabbed Gavigan in the arm, and Butler in the head.

Quimbo Appo ran to a Chinese boarding house, but he was soon found by the police hiding under a bed. After he was arrested, Quimbo Appo told the police, "Yes, I killed her."

The front page of the *Herald Tribune* read the following day, "Murder in the Fourth Ward."

Quimbo Appo's trial took place on April 11, 1859. It took the jury less than one hour to reach a guilty verdict. Even though the prosecutor, District Attorney Nelson J. Waterbury, recommended life imprisonment, a month later, Judge Davies sentenced Quimbo Appo to the death penalty. However, Quimbo Appo's lawyer appealed the case, and on May 8, 1860, Governor Morgan commuted Quimbo Appo's death sentence, and instead he gave him a 10-year term in the state penitentiary at Sing Sing in Ossining, New York.

However, because of Appo's penchant for violence, and also because he was basically a lunatic, Quimbo Appo's 10-year bit evolved into a life sentence. As a result of several violent incidents and bizarre behavior, Appo never again became a free man. He died at the Watteawan Hospital for the Criminally Insane on June 23, 1912.

After his father's incarceration, George Appo and his mother returned to their slum apartment on Oliver Street. Soon after, Catherine Appo decided to take her son and his younger sister on the ship *The Golden Gate,* to visit Catherine's brother in San Francisco. However, the ship was caught in a violent storm and sank. Both Appo's mother and his sister perished, but Appo somehow survived.

Appo wrote: "I cannot explain how I was saved, only that a sailor brought me to New York and left me with a very poor family named Allen."

The Allen family lived in the rear-yard tenement alley "Donovan's Lane," also called "Murderer's Alley." The alley was located on a tiny strip of hidden dirt, with the tenements so close together, hardly any daylight could penetrate into the alley.

Appo wrote: "One entrance was on Baxter and the other entrance was on Pearl Street. Poor people of all nationalities lived on this Donovan's Lane. It was a common sight to see every morning at least 6 to 10 drunken men and women sleeping off the effects of the five-cent rum bought at 'Black Mike's,' which was located at 14 Baxter Street. Next door to Mike's was a second-hand clothing store owned by a man named Cohen, who was a fence, where all the crooks used to get rid of their stolen goods. Above Cohen's store was where all the Chinamen of the city lived. At the time, there were only about 60 Chinamen in all New York City, and the lane was then called Chinatown."

Donovan's Lane was in the heart of New York City's worst slum called "The Five Points." Stuck in this cesspool of humanity, Appo learned the tricks of the trade that enabled him to make a decent living working in a life of crime.

Appo, at about the age of 10, became part of a group of scavengers, whom the people at that time called street urchins, street Arabs, street rats, or guttersnipes. While Appo was making an honest buck working at low-level jobs, like shining shoes, sweeping sidewalks, and selling newspapers, Appo also perfected his true love: the art of picking pockets.

It was quite easy for a young boy selling newspapers to pick the pocket of an unsuspecting mark. Appo used the guise of the "newspaper dodge": a ruse in which while he was ostensibly selling newspapers, Appo, with one hand, would wave the newspaper in a customer's face, and then with the other hand he'd pick the victim's pocket.

Appo's pickpocketing mentor was a master craftsman named Jim Caulfield. Caulfield once told a policeman, "If you will stand for a newspaper under your chin, I can take your watch, your watch and chain, and even your socks."

In the winter of 1871, Appo was caught picking the pocket of a downtown businessman. The businessman grabbed Appo by the neck and handed him off to a passing policeman saying, "This boy just robbed $28 from my vest pocket."

Appo pleaded guilty before Judge Joseph Dowling. The judge sentenced Appo to an undetermined time in a reform school, which was located on the naval vessel *The Mercury. The Mercury* housed 242 boys, who were convicted of such crimes as vagrancy, truancy, and larceny. On board *The Mercury,* boys learned seafaring skills, such as navigation, seamanship, military drills, and making different kinds of rope knots, which were essential in a seafaring life. There were also classes for the boys in reading, writing, and arithmetic.

Yet, life on *The Mercury* was anything but idyllic. The food was barely edible. The water was filthy, and contagious germs permeated the ship.

In 1872, the Mercury made a nine-month trip to and from Barbados. Upon returning to Harts Island off the coast of Manhattan, Appo and several other boys escaped from the vessel by lowering themselves by a rope to a rowboat. After they arrived on shore in downtown Manhattan, Appo hustled back to Donovan's Lane, and he commenced picking pockets again.

In 1874, Appo was caught by a policeman picking the pockets of a Wall Street executive. Appo tried to flee, but a passing detective followed him in hot pursuit, firing his pistol at Appo. Appo was hit once in the stomach, but he managed to escape.

Appo staggered into a building at 300 Pearl Street, and he went to an apartment that was occupied by the Maher family. While Mrs. Maher hid Appo under a bed, she ordered her son to go out in front of the apartment building to see if any policemen were in the area. When the coast was clear, Appo fled the apartment, and he received treatment at St. Luke's hospital from a physician who was friendly with one of Appo's confederates. The bullet in Appo's stomach was removed, and soon Appo was back on the streets doing what he had been doing before. Six months later, Apple was again caught picking pockets. He was tried, convicted, and sentenced to two years and six months in Sing Sing prison.

At Sing Sing, Appo was reunited with his father, who went in and out of lucidity. The senior Appo was normal on most days, but on his bad days, he was delirious and said things like "I am King of the World."

In Sing Sing, Appo was given a job in the laundry room as a "presser" of shirts. After Appo accidentally burned one of the shirts, Appo's teeth were knocked out by one of the guards. Then three guards took Appo to the guard room, handcuffed him from behind and forced him to lay face down on a paddleboard table. There Appo was given nine sharp lashes with an oar on his back and spine, rendering him unconscious.

When Appo regained consciousness, the head keeper said to him, "Do you think you can go back and do your work all right now? If you don't, we have a way to make you."

Appo told the keeper, "You punished me for nothing, and the

next time I am brought here you will punish me for something."

Appo stumbled back to the laundry shop. He immediately took the shirts that were on his table waiting to be ironed, and he put them in a hot stove where they soon were reduced to ashes. After his dirty deed was discovered, Appo was brought back to the guard room. When he was asked why he did what he had done, Appo refused to answer. Appo was immediately taken to one of the "dark cells," where he was imprisoned for 14 days. During those 14 days, Appo was given two ounces of bread and a glass of water every 24 hours.

After serving 30 months in Sing Sing, Appo was released on April 2, 1876. He immediately went back to picking pockets.

During the next eight years, Appo was arrested twice more for pickpocketing. Both times he was convicted and returned to prison; the last time on Blackwell's Island.

Appo escaped from Blackwell's Island by shimmying down a rope from the ship where he was working to the water down below. Appo jumped into a small rowboat, and he rowed until he docked in downtown Manhattan. Appo immediately sunk the boat, and he made his way to Mulberry Street where he was able to borrow some clothes.

The next day Appo absconded to Philadelphia.

Appo did very well picking pockets in Philadelphia. But the lure of his old haunts in downtown Manhattan, especially the opium dens, was too much to resist. Back in the Sixth Ward, Appo decided to deviate from his usual pickpocketing and engage himself in the flimflam business. Appo's chief swindle was giving store owners the wrong change for a $10 or $20 bill. This racket went fine for a while, until Appo was caught in a jewelry shop shorting the owner. However, through the machinations of the nefarious law firm of Howe and Hummel, Appo was somehow able to escape prison time.

In the early 1890's, catching pickpockets and flimflam men became the favorite pastime of the New York City police. So Appo decided to try a new scheme, a scheme in which he was less likely to be arrested. This scheme was called "The Green Goods Swindle."

The Green Goods Swindle was a three-pronged operation. It started with the "operators," or the bosses, who hired "writers," who wrote circulars to be sent to all parts of the country. The basis of these circulars was to entice people to agree to purchase counterfeit money. The green goods circular contained wording something similar to this:

"I am dealing in articles, paper goods – ones, twos, fives, 10's, and 20's – (do you understand?). I cannot be plainer until I know your heart is true to me. Then I will satisfy you that I can furnish you with a fine, safe, and profitable article that can be used in any manner and for all purposes, and no danger."

The writers would also include in the circular the prices for their goods. A typical price list read:

For $1,200 in my goods (Assorted) I charge $100. For $2,500 in my goods (Assorted) I charge $200. For $5,000 in my goods (Assorted) I charge $350. For $10,000 in my goods (Assorted) I charge $600."

These circulars were sent to people from around the country who had invested in various lotteries. The feeling of the operators was that these were the types of people who most likely would do something illegal for monetary profit.

Confederate soldiers were also sent circulars. New York City assistant district attorney Ambrose Purdy explained why.

"Former Confederates were so emotionally embittered and economically indebted, that they viewed green goods as a good way to hurt the government," Purdy said.

Once communication had been established between the "marks" and the operator, the marks were directed to take a train to New York City, or to the nearby suburbs. There the marks would meet the third cog in the Green Goods Swindle, who was called the "steerer."

The steerer, one of whom was George Appo, would meet the marks at the railroad station and take them to the operator, or the "turning point," who was waiting for the mark, either at a bogus storefront, or in a hotel room. The operator would show the marks a sample of his "counterfeit" money, which was actually legal tender. The mark, being satisfied that the money certainly looked legal, would give the operator the money that had been agreed upon to purchase the "queer bills."

The operator would then put the bogus counterfeit money into a cheap suitcase. A diversion would then occur, temporarily deflecting the mark's attention. During this diversion, the operator would switch the suitcase and replace it with an identical one given to him by one of his confederates. Of course, the second suitcase was filled with plain ordinary paper and sometimes even sand.

At this point, the job of the steerer was to get the mark quickly out of town, before the mark realized he had been swindled. As added insurance, the operator sometimes employed the services of a local cop or a detective, and sometimes even several local cops or detectives.

If the steerer had a problem with the marks, either on the way to the train station, or on the train before it left the station, the crooked lawman would jump in and threaten the mark with arrest if the mark didn't leave town immediately. The mark would have no recourse, since he had been attempting an illegal transaction in the first place.

One such green goods swindle almost cost George Appo his life.

In February 1893, Appo was working a green goods swindle with Jim McNally as his operator. Appo was directed by McNally to meet two men at a hotel in Poughkeepsie, New York. Appo went to the New York Hotel in Poughkeepsie, and he entered the room of two men named Hiram Cassel and Ira Hogshead, both shady entrepreneurs from North Carolina.

Appo gave the men a letter identifying Appo as the connection between the Old Gentleman (the operator) and the two men. Appo said that he would take the two men to the train station to board a train for Mott Haven, where they would see the counterfeit money they were purchasing. After the transaction was completed, Appo said he would take the men directly to the train station, pay their fare and send them on their way back home. Appo told the men that on the way to the train station, they must walk 10 feet behind Appo, and they must speak to no one, including Appo.

Appo arrived at the train station first, soon followed by Hiram Cassel. However, Ira Hogshead had stopped just short of the train station and was talking to a policeman; the same policeman who recently had a fallout with Jim McNally over his cut in a previous swindle.

Appo approached Hogshead and asked him why he was speaking to the policeman.

Hogshead said, "I don't care to do business. I've changed my mind."

Appo walked the men back to their hotel room, where Hogshead insisted the deal was done. Hogshead demanded that Appo leave the hotel room immediately, or there would be trouble.

Appo said he would do what Hogshead had requested, and as Appo was shaking Cassel's hand, Hogshead shot Appo in the right temple. Appo was taken to the hospital in critical condition. In a few days, Appo's right eye became infected and it had to be removed.

Cassel and Hogshead went on trial for the shooting of Appo. However, since Appo, true to the code of a "good fellow," refused to testify against the two men, which prompted the judge to release Cassel and Hogshead with a simple $50 fine. Appo, however, was arrested for running the green goods swindle, and he was sentenced to three years and two months at hard labor. In addition, Appo was fined $250.

Luckily for Appo, after spending only a few months in Clinton Prison, on November 28, 1893, the New York Court of Appeals overturned Appo's conviction.

Feeling betrayed by Jim McNally and by green goods operators in general, Appo agreed to testify before the Lexow Committee, which was looking into police corruption and police involvement in the green goods swindle in particular.

Appo didn't tell the committee anything they didn't already know, but he was branded a rat on the streets of New York City. As a result, Appo was shunned by the very people he had done business with for many years.

George Appo caught a break, when in September of 1894, he was approached by George W. Lederer, a renowned theater producer. Lederer offered Appo a part in his new play entitled "In the Tenderloin," in which Appo was to simply play himself, in a play about New York City's underbelly.

Appo toured the country in this play for several years, but when the play's run ended, Appo was stiffed by Lederer for $15,000 in unpaid salary. Although he tried for several years, Appo never did collect his money.

At the start of the 20th century, George Appo decided to live free of crime. He worked as a car cleaner at Grand Central Terminal, and also as a handyman at Calvary Church, the Sallade dress factory, and in the home of millionaire reformer Alexander Hadden.

In 1915, during the government's investigations of opium dens, Appo began secretly working for the government. Appo received a salary of six dollars a month, in addition to another six dollars a month for rent for his apartment. Soon, Appo's salary was increased to $10 a month.

In his final years, little was heard about George Appo. What is known, is that Appo lived in a small apartment in Hell's Kitchen on the west side of Manhattan.

On August 10, 1929, George Appo was admitted to the Manhattan State Hospital on Wards Island. By that time, Appo was nearly deaf and almost blind.

On May 17, 1930, even though he had been shot four times, stabbed twice (once in the throat) and brutally beaten in prison, George Appo died at the age of 73 from nothing more than old age.

Ah Hoon - The Murder of Chinese Comedian Ah Hoon

Sometimes a comedian can be dead funny, but after one of his onstage performances, Chinese comedian Ah Hoon turned up quite dead instead.

The Tong Wars started in Chinatown in 1899, with the powerful On Leong Tong dominating the gambling and drug interests in downtown Manhattan. The smaller Hip Sing and the Four Brothers Tongs joined forces and engaged in violent confrontations with the On Leong Tong, over the rights to control Chinatown's illegal activities. Almost daily, dead bodies littered the streets of Chinatown, which at the time only consisted of Mott Street, Pell Street, Chatham Square, and Doyers Street.

Ah Hoon was a famous Chinese comedian, who was featured often at the Chinese Theater at 5-7 Doyers Street, right in the middle of the Tong War Zone. The Chinese Theater was a venue, not only for the Chinese, but for English speaking audiences who were brave enough to venture into an area where gunpowder permeated the air. Ah Hoon was an associate of the On Leong Tong, and the content of his jokes, in which he constantly disparaged the Hip Sing and Four Brothers Tongs, made it seem like he thought he was bullet-proof.

Things started to get hairy for Ah Hoon, when the Reverend Huie Kim, the pastor of the Christian Morning Star Mission on Doyers Street, warned Ah Hoon that his jokes were not too funny with certain people. The good reverend also told Ah Hoon that Ah Hoon could get badly hurt if he kept telling his jokes on stage, where hundreds of people could hear the many indignities he spewed disparaging the Hip Sing and Four Brothers Tongs.

Ah Hoon thumbed his nose at the Reverend Huie Kim, and as a result, the Hip Sing and Four Brothers Tongs formally declared war on the On Leong Tong. Instead of holding back, Ah Hoon stepped up the frequency and the ferocity of his jokes on stage. This thoroughly annoyed the Hip Sing and Four Brothers Tongs, so they announced publicly that they were going to kill Ah Hoon. To make sure Ah Hoon got the message, they sent an emissary to Ah Hoon, giving him the exact time and date he was going to be murdered.

Ah Hoon took the threat with a shrug. But it was Hoochy-Coochy Mary, who lived on the floor below Ah Hoon, in a boarding house on Chatham Square, who ran to the police and begged them to protect the comedian. On December 30, 1909, Police Sergeant John D. Coughlin and two patrolmen accompanied Ah Hoon to his performance at the Chinese Theater. Word had spread quickly on the streets of Chinatown that Ah Hoon was scheduled to be murdered, and as a result, the theater was packed with people hoping to see a live execution for the price of a simple theater admission. Standing-room-only tickets were also sold out, and there was a huge crowd outside, not too happy at being turned away from witnessing Ah Hoon's dramatic demise.

Seeing the police presence, inside and outside the theater, the Hip Sing Tong decided to back away from their word, and at the end of the show, Ah Hoon, to the chagrin of the crowd, was still alive and joking. Sergeant Coughlin and his two underlings hustled Ah Hoon out of the theater, through a hidden underground tunnel, to his dwelling on Chatham Square. Ah Hoon climbed the stairs of his building, entered his room and locked the door. A group of heavily-armed On Leong bodyguards stood guard outside Ah Hoon's door, while dozens milled in the street outside his building looking for any impending attack. Ah Hoon went to sleep that night, but he did not wake up the following morning.

Hoochy-Coochy Mary heard a shot in the middle of the night, and she ran upstairs to alert the On Leong bodyguards. When they broke through the door, they found Ah Hoon dead on his bed with a bullet hole in his chest. What made the matter all the more vexing was that there was only one window in Ah Hoon's room and it faced a blank building wall five feet away.

The solution to Ah Hoon's death was quite simple and complicated at the same time.

So they wouldn't be seen by the On Leong bodyguards, the Hip Sing assassins had slipped into a tenement several buildings down from Ah Hoon's building. They climbed the stairs to the roof, then they jumped across three roofs to the roof of the building next to Ah Hoon's building. There they lowered the killer on a boatswain's chair tied to a rope, down the narrow alley, until he was parallel to Ah Hoon's window. The killer then quietly entered Ah Hoon's room and shot the Chinese comedian right through the heart. The deed being done, the killer exited the room in the same manner in which he had entered.

The Hip Sing Tong was so overjoyed at the success of their

mission, they held a parade the next day in the streets of Chinatown, complete with fireworks, ancestral music, and the dancing of the mythical Chinese dragons.

On New Year's night 1910, two days after the murder of Ah Hoon, the Chinese Theater was packed to the rafters again. In the middle of the performance, someone threw several packs of lit firecrackers into the air. People panicked, and they fled the theater quickly; except for five On Leong Tong members who were shot dead during the distraction of the fireworks.

No one was arrested for their murders, and the Tong Wars continued for another generation.

The Vicious Killing of Bow Kum

In 1899, the Tong Wars began in New York City's Chinatown, when the smaller Hip Sing and Four Brothers Tongs joined forces against the powerful On Leong Tong, in a battle for the immense illegal profits generated in Chinatown from gambling and drug dealing. There were sporadic killings throughout the first decade of the 20th Century, but the blood started flowing more rapidly in 1909. It was sparked by the vicious murder of a Chinese slave girl named Bow Kum, known as "The Little Flower."

In the Canton Region of China, Kum was sold by her father for a few paltry yen. She was then brought to the United States where she was sold at the slave-trade market in San Francisco, for the huge sum (at the time) of three thousand dollars. The buyer was Low Hee Tong, a high-ranking member of the Hip Sing and Four Brothers Tongs.

Kum lived with Tong for four years, but then the San Francisco police discovered the illegal servitude. When Tong could not produce a marriage license, Kum was taken away from Tong and placed in a Christian mission run by Donaldina Cameron, a Scotswoman famous for helping young Chinese slave girls escape from the terrible Tongs. Soon, gardener Tchin Lee, a member of the On Leong Tong, married Kum and took her to New York City.

Tong was furious he had lost the services of his female slave, but more furious over the loss of his three thousand dollars. As a result, Tong demanded that Lee give him back the money he spent on purchasing Kum.

Lee refused.

Tong then listed his grievances in a letter to the Hip Sing and Four Brother Tongs in New York City. Tong's Tongs agreed with him, and they demanded that the On Leong Tong force Lee to return Tong's money. Their request was denied, and immediately the Hip Sing and Four Brothers Tongs flew the red flag from their building on Pell Street, indicating they were declaring war against the On Leong Tong.

On August 15, 1909, a Hip Sing assassin broke into Lee's apartment at 17 Mott Street. The assassin stabbed Kum three times in the chest, cut off several of her fingers, and then mutilated her torso. This started a bloody war that resulted in over fifty killings in just a few short months.

In late 1909, Captain William Hodgins, the Commander of the 5th Precinct on Elizabeth Street, interceded, and he tried to make peace between the factions. He approached the On Leong Tong first, and they agreed to end the war, but only if the other two tongs gave them, as reparations, a Chinese flag, a roasted pig, and ten thousand packs of fireworks. The two smaller tongs considered this a huge insult, and the killings intensified for another year.

In late 1910, the United States government became involved. The Chinese Minister, in Washington D.C., appointed a committee of 40 Chinese merchants, teachers, and students to mediate the Tong Wars. An agreement was forged between the On Leong Tong, and the Hip Sing Tongs. However, the Four Brothers Tong refused to participate in the peace. As a result, the killings continued but not at the same pace as before.

Kerosene was thrown on the fire in 1912, when a new Tong, the Kim Lan Wui Saw Tong, suddenly appeared in New York City. In a battle for the illegal buck, these upstarts inexplicably declared war on the other three established Tongs. This was a dumb move, since the three older Tongs, instead of fighting among themselves, turned all their venom on the outmanned Kim Lan Wui Saw Tong.

The bodies continued to pile up in Chinatown, bringing outside business into the area to a halt. Finally, the Chinese government on mainland China, in conjunction with the New York City Police Department, compelled the warring factions to formally agree to halt the hostilities. The treaty was signed on May 22, 1913, by the Chinese Merchant's Association.

Since tourists were no longer afraid to enter Chinatown (and get caught in the cross hairs of the daily gunfire), peace and prosperity returned to the area.

That is, until 1924, when the bloody Tong Wars resumed.

Mock Duck

No, Mock Duck is not an item on the menu of a Chinese restaurant, but rather the name of one of the most notorious Chinese gangsters ever to set foot in America.

Real name, Sai Wing Mock, Mock Duck was born in China in 1879. In the late 1890's, Mock Duck traveled to the United States. He immediately took residence in New York City's Chinatown, where he joined the Hip Sing Tong, a small group of Chinese gangsters led by Lem Tong Sing.

At the time, Chinatown was controlled by the powerful On Leong Tong, whose boss was the murderous Tom Lee. Soon, Mock Duck pushed aside Lem Tong Sing as leader of the Hip Sing Tong, and he took control of the Tong himself. Mock Duck's first act as boss of the Hip Sing Tong was to demand fifty percent of the profits from Tom Lee's On Leong Tong. This did not sit well with Lee, and as a result, the Tong Wars of the early 1900's started in full force.

Mock Duck, knowing his Hip Sing Tong couldn't compete in terms of total gang members against the On Leong Tong, joined forces with the Four Brother's Society to even up the numbers a bit. Still, the Tong Wars became a bloody mess for three decades, with many casualties on all sides.

On January, 24, 1906, as a group of On Leong Tong members exited a building at 32 Pell Street, a dozen Hip Sing Tong members jumped from an alley on Doyers Street, and the fired as many as hundred rounds of ammunition at their rivals. Two On Leong Tong members were killed, and two were badly injured. This rampage was reportedly planned by Mock Duck, who ordered murders to be done, but very rarely got his hands dirty doing the actual killings himself.

The one exception was in 1900, when Mock Duck allegedly murdered a New Jersey tailor named Ah See, in front of 23 Mott Street. Mock Duck was tried three times for See's murder, but was never convicted.

Mock Duck lived in a top floor apartment with his family at 21 Pell Street, in the heart of Chinatown. The rest of the apartments in this building also housed Hip Sing Tong members. There had been several attempts on Mock Duck's life, so he was forced to wear a "chain mail" vest, in addition to always carrying two guns and a small hatchet for protection, just in case.

On January 12, 1912, Mock Duck narrowly escaped death, when two On Leong Tong members casually entered an apartment at 21 Pell Street. They opened fire at a group of Hip Sing Tong members, as the Hip Sings played a game of fan-tan, killing Lung You, one of Mock Duck's top henchmen. Luckily for Mock Duck, he was out of the building at the time and was not a victim of the shooting, which was obviously intended for him.

Mock Duck was finally arrested by the police in 1912 for the minor crime of running a "policy game," more commonly known as the "numbers racket." Mock Duck was convicted and sentenced to two years in Sing Sing Prison. When Mock Duck was released in 1914, he returned to Chinatown, and he assumed a very low profile in the Hip Sing Tong.

In 1932, Mock Duck briefly resurfaced in the news, when he, in conjunction with the American and Chinese governments, arranged a truce, officially ending the Chinatown Tong Wars.

Unlike most of his fellow Chinese Tong members, who were killed in the streets of Chinatown, Mock Duck died of natural causes, at the age of 72, in his Brooklyn home in 1941.

Steve Brodie

He was a hoaxer and a huckster, and the personification of what the Gay 90's Bowery/Chinatown area was all about. But no matter what legend says, Steve Brodie did not jump off the Brooklyn Bridge.

Steve Brodie was born in New York City on Christmas Day 1861. Not getting much of a school education, Brodie became a newsboy and then a bootblack, who eventually earned his living on the Manhattan side of the newly-constructed Brooklyn Bridge, which connected downtown Manhattan and the southern tip of Brooklyn.

The Brooklyn Bridge, built on the edge of Chinatown and completed in 1883, was designed by German immigrant John Augustus Roebling. It took 13 years to build, but Roebling did not live to see its completion. During the initial phase of construction, Roebling had his toes crushed, and after his foot was amputated a tetanus infection caused his death. The project was completed by his son Washington Roebling, who, after he too suffered a debilitating injury during the construction phase, was helped by his wife, Emily, who was basically the liaison between her bedridden husband and the construction crew on site.

When finished, the Brooklyn Bridge had a span of 1,595.5 feet, which at its grand opening, made it 50 percent longer than any other suspension bridge in the world. The bridge was 78 feet, six inches below water level and 276 feet six inches above water level. On the first day it opened, 150,300 people crossed the Brooklyn Bridge, along with 1,800 horse-drawn vehicles.

On May 30, 1883, one week after the bridge opened, a rumor spread that the bridge was about to collapse. People panicked, which led to a stampede in both directions. At least 12 people were killed and others not accounted for. After this tragic incident, people were afraid to cross the bridge. So, P.T. Barnum, of circus fame, removed all doubts, when on May 17, 1884, as a promotion for his circus, Barnum marched 21 elephants across the Brooklyn Bridge.

The first lunatic who tried to jump off the Brooklyn Bridge did not fare very well. In late May 1884, right after P.T. Barnum's successful stunt, swimming instructor Robert Emmitt Odlum, oddly enough the brother of women's rights activist Charlotte Odlum Smith, took a flying leap off the Brooklyn Bridge, and he went splat into the water. When Odlum's body floated to the surface, he was indeed quite dead.

By 1886, Steve Brodie was a man down on his luck. After betting on inferior horses at the racetrack, Brodie decided to make a winner out of himself by jumping off the Brooklyn Bridge. But Brodie was no fool. He knew what had happened to Odlum, and he took all precautions to make sure he didn't suffer the same fate.

On June 23, 1886, at approximately 2 p.m., Brodie stood at the entrance of the Brooklyn Bridge. According to the *New York Times* article the following day, Brodie had made a $200 bet to clear up his racetrack losses. The bet was that he would be brave enough to jump off the Brooklyn Bridge.

Before he got onto the bridge, Brodie kissed his wife goodbye.

She replied, "Good-bye Steve and take care of yourself. And may you be successful and scoop us dose $200, so that we kin have a good time."

According to published reports, Brodie then rode a wagon, which took him to the part of the Brooklyn Bridge just above the East River. In the water below, three men in a rowboat allegedly awaited Brodie's jump, so that they could fish him from the drink before he drowned. According to the *New York Times* article, Brodie took off his coat and hat, but not the rest of his clothes.

Someone yelled, "Police! Suicide! Look out! He's going to jump into the river!"

What happened next has been disputed for years; but in fact, no one who wasn't connected to the ruse had actually seen Brodie jump off the Brooklyn Bridge. What is certain, is that the three men in the rowboat rowed to where Brodie was floundering in the East River. When they got to Brodie, they dragged him by his shoulders into the rowboat. The men then rowed back to the pier on the Manhattan side of the Brooklyn Bridge, where they were met by Patrolmen Lally. Patrolman Lally immediately put Brodie under arrest.

"On what charge do you arrest me?" Brodie said.

"For jumping off the bridge and endangering your life," Patrolman Lally said. "You better come with me."

"OK, I'll go wid you, but I guess I'll get the $200," Brodie said.

"I can jump off de highest bridge in de world now."

Immediately, there were skeptics as to whether Brodie had actually jumped off the bridge; some argued it was all a stunt. Soon, word began circulating in the streets of Chinatown and the Bowery that Brodie had pulled off the caper, not for $200, but because a man named Moritz Herzberg had offered Brodie to buy him a saloon, on the basis that after the stunt, Brodie would be famous and so would his saloon.

Even though the *New York Times*, which employed two reporters who said they actually saw Brodie jump, reported Brodie's swan dive off the Brooklyn Bridge to be quite true, in fact they were all in on the caper. What really happened was this:

One of Brodie's confederates on the Brooklyn Bridge, upon receiving a signal from another accomplice on the dock, dropped a dummy loaded with iron clippings into the water below. At this point, Brodie was hiding under a pier in a small rowboat. As soon as the dummy hit the water, Brodie dove from the rowboat into the water, and he swam to the spot near where the dummy had sunk. Brodie's three pals in the rowboat rowed to where Brodie had swum, and they picked him up.

The rest is history.

Suddenly, a nobody named Steve Brodie became an instant star in New York City. Trying to cash in on his fame as much as he could, Brodie became the centerpiece of an exhibit at Alexander's Museum. To further inflate his fraudulent image, Brodie performed a series of stunts similar to the one he staged at the Brooklyn Bridge. In each stunt, Brodie was pulled from the water after a purported jump from a severe height, but not once did anyone not involved with Brodie actually see Brodie make the jump. After each stunt, Brodie received more newspaper coverage, which further amplified his daredevil image.

Brodie pulled one stunt too many, when after one faked jump, he disappeared completely, leading the suckers who bought Brodie's exploits in the first place to believe that he had died by drowning. When Brodie resurfaced in a Bowery bar a few weeks later, the newspapers figured they had been had, and they refused to give Brodie any more press coverage.

Brodie tried to resuscitate his image by actually trying to perform a stunt he said he would do. Brodie considered himself a strong swimmer, so he announced to the world he would swim the rapids in Niagara Falls. Dressed in a rubber suit, Brodie was lowered by a rope into the frigid waters. But as soon as Brodie's toes settled into the drink, panic set in. Brodie, in a frenetic state and figuring his daredevil days were over, begged to be pulled back into the boat by the rope. And that he was.

So much for Steve Brodie – daredevil.

Not being able to fool the public any longer, Brodie figured it was time take up Moritz Herzberg's offer of buying Brodie a saloon. In 1890, Brodie opened "Steve Brodie's Saloon" at 114 Bowery near Grand Street (the Bowery is the east boarder of Chinatown). The saloon became an immediate success with the sporting crowd. Boxing celebrities like John L. Sullivan, Jim Jeffries, James Corbett and Tom Sharkey (all of whom later would become world heavyweight champions) frequently hung out in Brodie's joint. Brodie was always on hand to shake a hand; sometimes even tending bar himself.

Behind the bar was a huge oil painting which showed Brodie courageously making his imaginary swan dive off the Brooklyn Bridge. To add veracity to a mendacious non-event, next to the oil painting was a framed affidavit signed by the "boat captain" who supposedly had fished Brodie from the East River.

Surrounding Brodie's oil painting were nonsensical signs, spouting such inanities as, "The Clock is Never Right," and "We Cash Checks For Everyone," and "$10,000 in the Safe To Be Given Away to the Poor," and "Ask the Bartender For What you Want," and finally, "If You Don't See What You Want, Steal It!"

Steve Brodie's Saloon consisted of three separate rooms. The front room was reserved for the neighborhood rabble who had swaggered inside for a cool libation. The two back rooms were for Brodie's pals and members of the press whom Brodie had on his pad.

And there were plenty of them.

The entire floor of all three rooms was inlaid with silver dollars, to give the impression that only the rich and mighty bent an elbow at Steve Brodie's Saloon, which was certainly not the case. But image is everything, so Brodie kept the press up to their gills in booze, and he stuffed a few bucks in their pockets to boot.

Tour buses made Steve Brodie's Saloon one of their must stops (Brodie paid the tour bus drivers well too).

As soon as the tour bus arrived in front, the tour guide would proudly proclaim, "Ladies and Gentlemen, you are seeing one of the most historic scenes in this great city. That, ladies and gentlemen, is Steve Brodie's Famous Saloon. You have all heard of Steve Brodie, the man who made that terrible leap for life from the Brooklyn Bridge to the East River below and lived to tell about it."

CA-CHING!

Soon, the entire tour bus crowd rushed inside Steve Brodie's Saloon to see a piece of history, and of course, to spend a few bucks buying Steve Brodie's booze.

Every once in a while, when the mood hit him, Brodie would wear a tattered suit, which he claimed was the exact one he was wearing when he made his "fearless jump." Then, if someone bought a round of drinks (and someone always did), Brodie, his chest puffed out a full two feet, would solemnly regale the crowd with a blow-by-blow description of his gallant leap into the murky waters of death.

Quite frankly, Steve Brodie had no shame.

In 1894, Steve Brodie, still trying to capitalize on his ill-founded fame, appeared in a play called *On the Bowery*, staring, of course - Steve Brodie. The play originally was conceived to star a local 5-foot-2-inch pugilist called "Swipes the Newsboy" (real name Simon K. Besser). However, Swipes accidentally killed a fellow boxer in the ring, which subsequently landed him in jail, because at the time boxing was illegal in New York City. So in stepped Steve Brodie, and the part was rewritten to accommodate Brodie's interesting life.

The play opened in Philadelphia, made a stop in Brooklyn, and then finally found its home at The People's Theatre at 199 Bowery, right down the street from Steve Brodie's Saloon. The play was basically a hokey mess of disjointed scenes, one of which took place in an exact replica of Steve Brodie's Saloon. Predictably, at the play's climax, Steve Brodie jumped off the Brooklyn Bridge to save the heroine named Blanch, who had been hurled into the frigid waters of the East River by the wretched villain Thurlow Bleekman.

In *On the Bowery* Brodie even got a chance to display his singing talents, or lack thereof. His heart-rendering rendition of *My Pearl* caused tears to flow from theatergoers' eyes. The words of which were:

My Pearl is a Bowery girl,

She's all the world to me,
She's in it with any girls 'round the town,
And a corking good looker, see?
At Walhalla Hall she kills them all,
As waltzing together we twirl.
She sets them all crazy, a spieler, a daisy,
My Pearl's a Bowery girl.

Applause!! Applause!! No tomatoes, eggs, or shoes, please. This is a respectable establishment.

With the play a resounding success, Steve Brodie's Saloon was even more popular than before. With his newfound wealth, Brodie substantially upgraded his attire. Brodie now lorded over his saloon resplendent with a five-carat diamond ring on his finger, diamond studs instead of buttons on his shirt, and a gold watch and chain, hooked onto his belt loop and slipped into his front pants pocket.

But alas, Brodie's wealth and success were short-lived.

On January 31, 1901, Steve Brodie died from complications due to diabetes. The man who had "jumped" from the Brooklyn Bridge was only 40 years old when he left this earth.

However, after Brodie's death he became more famous than ever before. Not wanting to disparage a dead man's name, the rumors of Brodie's chicanery concerning the Brooklyn Bridge dive became almost non-existent. In fact, a new American phrase was coined: "Pulling a Brodie," or, "Taking a Brodie," which meant doing something dangerous, or maybe even suicidal.

In 1933, Hell's Kitchen actor George Raft portrayed Brodie in *The Bowery,* a film directed by Raoul Walsh. In this movie, Raft (Brodie) attempts to stage a fake jump off the Brooklyn Bridge. With a crowd of 100,000 people congregated at the bridge, and with a dummy all set to be thrown in the river, the dummy inexplicably disappears.

Raft's young accomplice, aptly named Swipes (played by child actor Jackie Cooper) tells Raft, "They were hip to us so they copped it."

Raft shrugged his shoulders, and not wanting to disappoint the panting crowd, he made the daring jump into the drink himself.

And to the applause of the crowd, George Raft (Steve Brodie) survived.

Kiddies, this happens only in the movies.

Chuck Connors – The Un-Elected Mayor of Chinatown

Chuck Connors was a scam artist of the highest caliber and the most famous white man in Chinatown history. Because of his gregarious nature, Connors was called the "Mayor of Chinatown," even though Chinatown had its own elected Chinese Mayor, Tom Lee, the leader of the On Leong Tong.

George Washington "Chuck" O'Connor claimed he was born on Mott Street in Chinatown, but most likely was born in 1852 in Providence, Rhode Island.

Telling the truth was never Connors's strong point.

When Connors was a teenager, he changed his last name from O'Connor to Connors. Rumor had it that "Connors" had less of an Irish ring to it than "O'Connor," and the Irish were strongly associated with the police for whom Connors had no fondness.

Connors's early nickname in Chinatown, for some reason, was "Insect," but he soon was called "Chuck" by everyone, because he loved to cook chuck steaks by hoisting them on a stick and searing them over small fires he set in the streets of the Bowery and Chinatown. At various times in his wacky life, Connors was also called the "Sage of Doyers Street," and the "Bowery Philosopher."

As a young boy, Connors enjoyed tormenting the Chinese men by pulling on their pigtails, and then making his getaway by sprinting through the streets, usually with an angry Chinaman chasing him with a big knife. As a teenager, Connors learned to speak Chinese, which eventually endeared him to the Chinatown population.

As he grew older, Connors became a professional pugilist, and then a bouncer at Scotchy Lavelle's joint at 6 Doyers Street. Connors also frequented Tom Lee's dive at 9 Bowery, affectionately called "The Dump," which was said to have "the dirtiest species of white humanity ever to be found." (Strangely enough, even though there were dozens of bars in the Chinatown area, some even owned by Chinese men like Tom Lee, hardly any Chinese people frequented these places, preferring opium dens as their mode of relaxation and inebriation.)

During this time, Connors palled around with a Chinatown street thug named Big Mike Adams. Whereby Connors was playfully mischievous concerning his actions with the short and slim Chinese male population, Adams was downright deadly. Working as an enforcer for the local tongs, Adams bragged he killed a slew of Chinamen by decapitating them with his huge knife. Once in full view of dozens of witnesses, Adams forced three Chinamen onto their knees in broad daylight. Then, as the crowd screamed in horror, he decapitated them one by one. Adams's big piece of work was when, working for a rival tong, he decapitated Hip Sing Tong leader Ling Tchen.

After it became clear Adams was out of control, Connors kept his distance. As Adams became more belligerent against the Chinese, Connors developed a closer relationship with them. Adams lost much face when he was attacked on Pell Street by a drunken Hip Sing gangster named Sassy Sam. Adams, supposedly a tough guy, ran through the Chinatown streets screaming like a little girl, as Sassy Sam, swinging a Chinese ceremonial sword, chased Adams. This sign of weakness was Adams's undoing.

A few weeks later, Adams was found gassed to death in his Chinatown apartment. With the windows and doors in Adams's room closed off, someone had inserted a small rubber tube into the room's keyhole. The rubber tube was attached to an open gas jet in the hallway. That someone was believed to have been Chuck Connors, who did the job as a favor to his Chinese friends.

After Adams's death, Connors decided that maybe the streets of Chinatown were not too safe for him anymore. Adams had friends in Chinatown, and Connors heard rumors that they were gunning for him. His incessant drinking was also a hindrance to Connors's health, so Connors moved uptown to start a new life.

No drinking. No doping. No more heavy-handed work.

Soon, Connors met a woman he liked named Nellie, and he married her. To support himself and his wife, Connors took a job as a conductor on the Third Avenue El. During this period of marital bliss, Nellie taught Connors how to read and write.

But alas, the education of Chuck Connors came to an abrupt end, when Nellie died suddenly. As a result, Connors went back deep into the bottle. One day Connors got so drunk, he was shanghaied onto a ship, which set sail for London, England.

In London, Connors escaped his captors and hid in the inner city of Whitechapel. Connors made friends with the local costermongers, who were people who sold fish and produce from street stands and carts.

Connors absorbed and copied the local culture, and when he returned to his old New York City haunts, he was dressed smartly in the costermonger attire of bell-bottom trousers, blue striped shirt, yellow silk scarf, and a blue pea coat, resplendent with big pearl buttons, which also traveled down the seams of his trousers.

Connors's transformation included a little song he had learned on the other side of the pond:

Pearlies on my front shirt,
Pearlies on my coat,
Little bit of dicer, stuck up on my nut,
If you don't think I'm de real thing,
Why, tut, tut, tut.

The "little bit of dicer" Connors wore on his head was a derby two sizes too small, instead of the traditional costermonger cap which was frowned upon by the Bowery residents.

It was around this time that Connors became a bit of an eccentric (if he wasn't one already). With no visible means of support, Connors became best pals with *Police Gazette* publisher Richard K. Fox. Fox owned a row of buildings on Doyers Street, and he let Connors live at 6 Doyers Street rent free, as long as Fox could regale his readers with the real and imagined exploits of "The Great Chuck Connors." Fox even co-wrote Connors' autobiography called *Bowery Life*, in which he called Connors the "Mayor of Chinatown," which solidified Connors's reputation for life.

According to Luc Sante's wonderful book about the underbelly of New York City entitled *Low Life*, Fox's writings about Connors "was included in a series that otherwise ran mostly to boxing, wrestling, club-swinging, and poker manuals, was illustrated with photographs of Chuck in typical costume, striking poses (cigar in corner of mouth; one hand pointing forward with index, or back with thumb; the other hand in coat pocket with thumb sticking out; legs set apart, one forward, one back; pail of beer at the ready)."

The text of Fox's writings is dotted with many of Connors's

unique colloquialisms, such as:

> *Here's to me new graft. I'm one of dose guys now wot gits
> ink all over his flippers and looks wise. Say, it's a cinch,
> and I've got some of dem blokes wot writes books skinned
> a mile.*

Or, Connors's musings on what he would do if he became a
millionaire:

> *Me headquarters would be de Waldorf, but I would hev a
> telephone station in Chinatown, so I could get a hot chop
> suey w'en I wanted it quick. Ev'ry mornin' at 10 o'clock – or
> near dere – I'd call up me Chat'am Square agent an' tell
> him ter give cologne ter der gals an' segars an' free lunch ter
> der gorillas. Ev'ry bloke dat wuz hungry would have a feed
> bag an w'enever he wanted it. How does dat grab yer?*

With no visible means of legal support, Connors had to find
himself a quick way to make a buck. And he did so by becoming,
what was called in those days, a "lobbyglow": Chinese slang for
"tour guide." Connors worked the Bowery area, where there was
some competition for his services. However, Chinatown, because of
Connors's closeness to the Chinese leaders, was Connors's exclusive
territory. No other lobbyglow would dare enter Chinatown with his
customers.

Connors specialized in what was called "the vice tour," where
Connors would take his customers to seedy venues to witness the
depravity of the Bowery and Chinatown. While other lobbyglows
took any curiosity seeker who could pay the freight, Connors,
because of his fame as the Mayor of Chinatown, specialized in
bringing celebrities from all walks of life on his tours. Some of
Connors's customers included Sir Thomas Lipton, novelists Israel
Zangwell and Hall Caine, actors Henry Irving, Ellen Terry, and
Anna Held, and Swedish and Danish royal families. Of course,
because of Connors's cache in the Chinatown and Bowery areas, he
was able to charge higher prices than his competition, especially to
the swells just noted who could certainly afford it.

During Connors's "vice tour," he would regale his customers

with stories of hatchet murders and white slavery. But the highlight of Connors's tour was when he showed his customers the inside of a real-life opium den. These dens, of which Connors had several, were, in fact, total fakes. Connors employed several Chinese accomplices to stage his fabrications.

Two of Connors's cohorts were George Yee and his wife Blond Lulu. As soon as Connors gave them the secret knock on the door signaling his impending entrance with his crew, George and Lula would fake a drug-induced stupor, while smoking something purported to be opium, complete with the exotic aromas.

Then, as the tourists watched in amazement, Connors's assistant would proceed with a solemn monologue, spoken through a megaphone, saying, "These poor people are slaves to the opium habit. And whether you came here or not to see them, they would have spent the night smoking opium as you see them doing it now!"

Then on cue, Yee would stop smoking and stagger to his feet. Yee would start dancing slowly, gyrating his body in a suggestive way, while singing a little ditty entitled *Alle Samee Jimmy Doyle*. Connors would tell his enthralled customers that this was unimpeachable evidence that Yee had become crazed due to the effects of his non-stop opium smoking.

Then without another word, Connors would lead his crew out of the apartment to a Chinese restaurant, which would complete that particular tour. Meanwhile, George and Blond Lulu would tidy up and get ready for the next go-around, which took place in just a few hours.

Another duo of opium-smoking fakes, whom Connors employed was a prostitute named "Chinatown Gertie" and her partner (pimp?) Charlie Lee. Gertie's brothel was located at 12 Pell Street, right above "Nigger Mike's" Pelham Saloon. When Gertie was informed her apartment would be on Connors's tour that day, she immediately canceled any appointments with "customers," and turned her brothel into a phony opium-smoking den. The only problem was, that instead of smoking opium, which would have been safer, they smoked molasses, which caused Charlie Lee's premature demise.

When Connors was at the height of his fame, he started the Chuck Connors Association, which was for the benefit of (you guessed it) Chuck Connors himself. The sole purpose of the Chuck Connors Association was to throw a yearly gala that was attended by all the local politicians, millionaires, and members of most of the city's illustrious clubs, including the Princeton Club and New York Athletic Club, and by anybody in New York City who was somebody.

In December 1903, Connors held his yearly gala in Tammany Hall on East 14th Street. The joint was jumping with such celebrities as pugilists John L. Sullivan, James J. Corbett and Jim Jeffries (who was accompanied by actress Anna Held), French actress Maxine Elliot, as well as millionaire industrialist George F. Train. The music was provided by two bands: Professor Wolf's Orchestra, and to throw a bone to Connors's Chinatown connections, Professor Yee Wah Lung's Chinese Orchestra.

At the time, Connors's main squeeze was a charming gal named "Pickles," who was known as the "Belle of Chinatown." While Connors was busy running the festivities, Pickles, a tall and buxom broad, arrived at the party around 11 p. m., accompanied by Ling Quong, the owner of a Chinatown opium den, who barely topped out at five feet tall. Both were a little high on something, liquid or otherwise.

Immediately, Pickles caused a stir at the ball, when she asked a passing older lady, who had her nose up in the air and was in the company of several gentlemen, "Hey sis, have you got any cigarettes?"

The lady stiffened and tried to barge past Pickles, but Pickles would have none of that.

Pickles grabbed the lady by the arm and pulled her back. "Go on and give me a pipe. Don't mind dem guys you wid. Give me the pipe!"

The lady sniffed at Pickles, "My poor girl, I don't smoke cigarettes."

Pickles thought about giving the lady the back of her hand. But then she reconsidered and said, "Back to der woods for yours!"

The lady and her male crew scurried away.

Looking around, Pickles realized she was greatly under-dressed for the upcoming march, in which she was supposed to be accompanying Connors. So she conned a young girl, with some loose change no doubt, to lend her the skirt the girl was wearing.

While Pickles was in the dressing room changing and sprucing up a bit, Connors began asking around as to Pickles's whereabouts.

A young girl in a pink dress told Connors, "My sister Mamie is lending her a blue skirt. Mamie will stay in the dressing room until the march is over."

Minutes later, Pickles made her grand entrance, resplendent in the borrowed skirt which was about six inches too short. She sauntered over to Connors who was waiting not too patiently, flipped her cigarette to the floor, and then snapped at Connors, "Come on Chuck, yer needn't be ashamed of me. I'd be the best looking rag in the hall."

Connors apparently agreed. He took Pickles by the arm and marched her around the hall, followed by 300 or so well-lit celebrants.

The joint was really jumping, when Carrie Nation made her unexpected and unwelcome appearance. Nation was a highly viable and quite loquacious member of the Ladies Temperance Movement, which opposed alcohol in pre-Prohibition America, as well as the notion of women smoking cigarettes. Nation was quite an imposing figure, standing over six-feet tall and weighing in the neighborhood of 175 pounds. If she were a boxer, male or female, Carrie Nation would certainly have been a heavyweight.

At first, Nation was stopped at the door by the bouncers, but Connors, obviously slightly in the bag himself, went to the door and said, "Sure she can come in. Der are udder automobiles upstairs with loose wheels. Jist step in and help yourself to a twist."

That was a big mistake.

Nation immediately stampeded past Connors, and she hustled to the bar area, where she saw several girls smoking cigarettes. Nation smacked the cigarettes from the girls' hands and did the same thing to their male counterparts.

"I came here to stop this ball!" Nation bellowed to the crowd. "I received a letter from a heartbroken mother about it, and she said her son lost his job by attending it last year. I'm going to break it up!"

Her face beet red, Nation approached a table where ladies were sitting with alcoholic drinks in front of them. Nation brushed the drinks off the table, and she told the startled ladies, "You ought to be arrested for drinking!"

Then Nation hurried to the main stage, climbed the steps, and proceeded to read a letter she had received, begging her to stop the Chuck Connors Association Ball.

Connors ordered the band to drown her out by playing a popular song named *Bedilia*. The crowd started singing, *"Bedilia, I'd like ter steal yer."*

Nation stood on the main stage, dumbfounded, as another segment of the crowd started chanting, "Put her out! Rats! Rats! Shut her up! Hey! Hey! Hey!"

By this time, Connors knew he had to do something, so he went to the main stage and induced Nation to leave the stage. Connors walked Nation toward the back door, and he told her, "I'd like to introduce you to a little girl who ought to be home in bed."

Outside, waiting under the steps leading to the back exit, was none other than Pickles, who screamed up at Nation, "If yer don't git down the stairs in a minute, I'll push your nose through the back of yer neck!"

Pickles hurried up the steps, and she grabbed Nation by the throat. Connor grabbed both women in a bear hug, and with the help of three bouncers, Carrie Nation was evicted from the premises.

After Nation was safely outside, Connors snapped at her, "The street is all yours!"

On May 10, 1913, Chuck Connors returned to his room at 6 Doyers Street, not feeling too chipper. He told Mrs. Chin, who had cared for him the past few years, "I'm not good for several more days."

Mrs. Chin immediately summoned Connors's pals from the Chatham Club. When they arrived at Connors's room, Connors told them, "If I am going to cash it in, let it be here in Chinatown."

Cooler heads prevailed, and Dr. Shields, from the Hudson Street Hospital, was immediately summoned. When he arrived at Connors's bedside, Dr. Shields discovered that Connors had a severe case of pneumonia. Connors was rushed to the nearby "House of Relief," where he died a few hours later at the age of 61.

Connors's funeral procession was one of the finest in Chinatown history. The procession started in front of Connors's residence at 6 Doyers Street. It consisted of 63 coaches filled with Connors's mourning friends and an additional six coaches stuffed with floral arrangements.

The mourners were a veritable who's who in the political world, the sporting world, and even the underworld. The only relatives in attendance were Connors's brother, Philip O'Connor, and Connors's sister, Mrs. Elizabeth (O'Connor) Miller.

The procession snaked through the streets of Chinatown, and then it stopped at Transfiguration Church at 29 Mott Street, for Connors's funeral mass, which was said by Father McCann. After the mass, the procession again wound around the streets of Chinatown and the Bowery. As Connors's coffin moved past each establishment, Chinese merchants set off their traditional funeral firework displays, in honor of a white man they considered one of their own.

The funeral procession continued over the newly-built Manhattan Bridge, and it ended at Calvary Cemetery in Queens, where Connors was finally interred.

Johnny Keyes – The Elected Mayor of Chinatown

In 1924, just as the area was being transformed from the Five Points into Little Italy/Chinatown, my uncle Johnny Keyes (real name Canonico – he married my mother's oldest sister, Mary) was re-elected the Mayor of Chinatown for a second time term by a paper-thin margin.

According to the June 21st, 1924 issue of the *New York Times*, my uncle's opponent was Le Chung Wei. But with the backing of New York City Mayor, John Francis Hyland, "Red Mike" to his pals, Johnny Keyes came out on top by a whopping 67 votes out of more than 4,500 votes cast. World heavyweight champion Jack Dempsey also contributed mightily, in the form of greenbacks, to my Uncle Johnny's campaign.

In his youth, Keyes was a professional boxer, but he was never more than a pleasing club fighter. Keyes also managed and trained over 100 fighters, including my mother's brother and Johnny Keyes's brother-in-law – Oakie Keyes (real name Daniel Mucerino). Five of Johnny Keyes's fighters, Pepper Martin, Chalky Wright, Archie Moore, Kid Chocolate, and Midget Wolgast became world champions.

Explaining how Johnny "Keyes" Canonico, an Italian/American, came to become the Mayor of Chinatown, the *New York Times* said:

> *The Mayor was born on Bayard Street when it was called the Five Points. He was a local leader from public school days and was deemed the heir-apparent to the late Chuck Connors in the latter part of Connors's administration. When Chuck died 12 years ago, Chinatown regarded Johnny as the logical successor.*

The *Times* went on further to explain how the 1924 election came about in the first place.

> *There is no fixed tenure of office for Chinatown Mayor. An election takes place any time an aspirant feels that he's*

strong enough to cope with the administration. A date for the election is fixed, and at a number of secret polling places, the ballots are marked and counted. Those known to the clerks of the polls as natives of Chinatown and its immediate confines are enfranchised.

After winning re-election, Uncle Johnny Keyes explained his mayoralty duties to the *New York Times* in his inimitable linguistic style, which was peppered with hyperbolic New York City slang:

This is a big job and you can't expect to keep regular hours at it. The Mayor of Chinatown has to sleep with his clothes on. He must be ready at any hour to rush to help Mrs. Grogan keep the old man from throwing the dinner table out of the window. When an argument between children on Mulberry Bend spreads to their parents, he must be able to keep the scratches and bruises down to as few as possible. In other words, he must keep the paddy wagons and ambulances out of Chinatown.

The Chinese don't get into too many scraps. They are hardworking and happy if they are left alone. Occasionally they have a dispute over a business matter, and this comes to me for settlement. If one steals the customer of another by giving a lower price, I am asked to stop the cutthroat competition. If a Chinaman is slow in making payments on something he bought from another Chinaman, I am asked to speed up the installments. This doesn't happen often because the Chinese are particular about paying debts.

However, according to Johnny Keyes, the most important job of the Mayor of Chinatown was to polish the bright image of the neighborhood and not let it be tarnished by outside influences.
Johnny Keyes told the *Times*:

We have no objection is people want to see a little of Oriental life in Chinatown. But we don't want the place held up as a nest of opium dens. As mayor, I have fought to keep the moving pictures companies from using scenery in Chinatown

*in plays in which the Chinese are villains and white girls get
kidnapped.*

*Of late, Chinatown has wanted its Mayor to give the
neighborhood a better reputation in the eyes of the rest of the
world. My men listen to the talk handed out by the guides on
the sight-seeing busses, and when it gets a little too harsh we
step in and tell them to stop.*

*The truth is there are probably fewer guns to a block in
Chinatown than anywhere else in the city. The days of the
hatchet men are gone, and there hasn't been a knife thrown
in years.*

Johnny Keyes also told the *Times*, that his responsibilities as
Mayor of Chinatown included helping the local parents control their
wayward offspring.
He said:

*Speaking to the young men who appeared headed to the
Tombs is another of my duties. Parents whose boys are in
bad company ask me to tell the kids they are making a
mistake. The young fellows listen. I have spoken with
hundreds of boys who have found it easier to steal than to
work and have managed to save most of them from getting in
bad.*

One of Johnny Keyes first actions after being re-elected
Mayor was to throw a grand shindig at Tammany Hall, which he
called the Chinatown 400 Ball. The expressed purpose of the events
was to raise substantial cash, intended strictly for the pockets of
Johnny Keyes, after he, of course, threw a few monetary bones to the
Tammany Hall brass (Keyes got this idea from his mentor, the dearly
departed Chuck Connors).
There was said to be almost 1,500 guests at the ball, and the
highlight of the night was a grand procession scheduled for 12
midnight, which was supposed to be led by the famous writer,
Damon Runyon, Keyes's close friend. But Runyon forgot to wear his
tuxedo to the ball, and a Tammany Hall bootlicker was sent by taxi

to fetch Runyon's tuxedo, which was at his upper West Side apartment.

The bells rang, signaling 1 a.m., and still there was no tuxedo. At 1:30 a.m., a member of the Chinatown 400 floor committee rushed up to the Silver Slipper Box, where Runyon and Keyes were holding court, and said that the taxi with Runyon's tuxedo and come and gone, but no one from Tammany Hall had been there to take possession of the formal wear.

Disgusted, Runyon turned to Keyes and said, "This is your ballgame now, Pally. I'm drunk, my belly is full, and I'm off to grander places."

"Hey, Cousin, you can't do that (Keyes called everyone Cousin or 'Cuz')!" Keyes said.

"Watch me," Runyon said.

And the next thing Johnny Keyes saw was Runyon's back shrinking in the distance.

According to the *Brooklyn Eagle*, Johnny Keyes was nonplused, and he decided to lead the grand march himself, accompanied by his lovely wife, Mary (this writer's aunt).

The *Eagle* wrote under the headline:

Chinatown Ball Joyous
But Damon Runyon Misses "Tux"
and Disappoints.
Was Scheduled to Lead March.
Oriental Setting Lacks Nothing but
Chinamen

Promptly at 2 o'clock, Johnny Keyes, Mayor of Chinatown, stepped down from his box to lead the march for the guests. Mrs. Keyes, in white georgette (sheer silk) embroidered in gold, was at his side, affecting one of the novelty Poiret dolls.

Huge bouquets of American Beauty roses were the favors of the evening. The stately march was followed by the song "Chinatown." Its jazz not only kept the dancers on the floor, but several went atop tables to give exhibitions of the art decried by the generation not familiar with its movements.

The imposing headdress of the Chinatown 400, said to have cost $4 each, gave the wearer a dignity alike to a potentate of the Mystic Shrine and a Chinese Mandarin.

Everybody had a wonderful time. Empty square bottles were everywhere.

And Johnny Keyes made a mint.

Besides being a savvy politician, Johnny Keyes fancied himself as somewhat of an entrepreneur, and an international one at that.

In 1925, with the backing of several prominent Chinese businessmen, Keyes traveled to the Canton region of China with several of his world-class fighters, including lightweight Pepper Martin, flyweight Mickey Nelson, and bantamweight Terry Martin, ostensibly to teach the locals the refinements of boxing.

But, as usual, Johnny Keyes had ulterior motives.

Keyes told the *New Castle Herald* in New Castle, Pennsylvania, "The Chinks are deficient, if one might not say utterly lacking in pep. A few smacks on the whiskers may stir up something in the fight business there, and then I'll be the only fight manager on the spot."

But, alas, Johnny Keyes's trip to China was also deficient, if one might not say utterly lacking in pep.

The idea of an American promoter staging boxing matches in China was slapped down by Chinese officials. And when Keyes proposed to the United States authorities that he should be allowed to import several Chinese boxers into the United States, he ran into the exclusion law - the Geary Act - or as it was previously called "The *Act to Prohibit the Coming of Chinese Persons into the United States* of May 1892."

This act of Congress said that only Chinese laborers would be allowed to shuffle back and forth between China and the United States, and not too many of them at that. So, try as he may, Johnny Keyes, the revered New York City "Mayor of Chinatown," and blessed with the gift of gab, could not convince immigration officials on either continent that the gaggle of Chinese boxers he wanted to bring to New York City's Chinatown could be in anyway categorized as "laborers."

As for the tens of thousands of dollars Keyes spent on his trip to China; which was, of course, other people's money, Keyes was again philosophical.

Upon returning empty-handed to Chinatown, Keyes told the Chinese businessmen who had financed his excursion, "It ain't your life. It ain't your wife. It's only money."

In 1926, Johnny Keyes had the bright idea of changing his name to Joe Russo, in order to confuse the prohibition agents, who were constantly breathing down his neck for the fact that his speakeasy, "The Dugout," at 58 Mulberry Street was serving illegal liquor.

"Why are the agents picking on me?" Keyes asked his brother John. "They say there's over 30,000 speakeasies in New York City. Why does my number come up every few fuckin' days?"

In January of 1926, Joe Russo/Keyes was picked up in the borough of Brooklyn for public intoxication. This was the third time in the past seven days that Russo had been put in a Brooklyn clink for staggering around the Borough of Kings smashed. It may have been a coincidence that The Dugout was shut down by prohibition agents the day before his first arrest.

When Russo arrived at the Brooklyn station house, he asked to make one phone call, which he did to his brother, John, who lived down on Bayard Street in the Five Points. When John arrived at the Brooklyn station house, according to January 25th, 1926 edition of *The New York World News Service*, "He became so abusive of the police, he was arrested, too."

On January 6, 1931, Johnny Keyes's nightclub, "The Dugout" at 58 Mulberry Street was forced to close its doors.

During the heights of Prohibition, The Dugout was the most widely visited speakeasy on the Lower East Side of Manhattan. World Heavyweight champion Jack Dempsey was a regular, as were Hollywood stars, James Cruze, Richard Dix and Richard Barthelmess, who was nominated for the first Academy Award for Best Actor in 1929 for his exploits in "The Patent Leader Kid" (1927) and "The Noose" (1928).

He won for neither.

Jimmy Durante got his start at "The Dugout," as did Irving Berlin, who was a singing waiter. Al Jolson and Eddie Cantor, both born on the Lower East Side, came to The Dugout often, and invariably they wound up on stage crooning the greatest hits of that era.

The day after the front door was boarded shut, Keyes, still the Mayor of Chinatown, was approached by a reporter from the *New York Sun,* who was able to enter The Dugout from an unlocked side door. This was just months after, the Bank of the United States defaulted and closed, costing Johnny Keyes the staggering sum of $15,000.

Asked why The Dugout was no more, Keyes told *The Sun,* "It ain't Prohibition; it was the Depression that killed me. And when the bank defaulted, I lost my 'rainy day' money."

Yet, Keyes promised there would soon be a reincarnation of The Dugout. But his math was slightly off when he told the *Sun,* "The décor going to be half Chinese, half Italian, and half American. And they'll be two Chinese at the gate, pigtails and all. The old joint was too small anyway. And it was old. The new joint is going to be somethin' else."

Keyes had grandiose ideas for his new nightspot, which he claimed would be heard on the radio by millions of people throughout the United States of America.

"I'm going to be the Master of Ceremonies, as usual, in my old slang way," Keyes said. "And we are going to be on the air all over the country. You know, we got 25,000 letters from all over the country from the broadcasting we did last winter. I had 'em as far west as Portland, Oregon, and we weren't using all that much power either."

Raising advertising money during the Depression was a bit of a problem, but as always, Johnny Keyes had an angle.

"We'll probably have a big bus uptown around Times Square tagged out with a big sign saying 'The Mayor of Chinatown's Dugout,'" Keyes said. "And it will be a real Chinese joint too. It will be the only Oriental place in this section of the Five Points. No meatballs and spaghetti like before. Strictly Peking Duck and friend rice, with eggrolls on the side. Close your eyes, and you'd think you were on Pell Street."

When the reporter asked how Keyes's boxing promoter's career was fairing since the stock market crash of 1929, Keyes said, "Boxing's gone; wrestling is the game now. But I'm still biding my time now. Boxing will come back, and I'll be in the pink again."

After the *Sun* reporter turned to leave, Keyes yelled at his back, "Come around when the new joint's opened. It's going to be some honky-tonk!"

After my beloved Aunt Mary passed away at a-much-too-young age, Johnny Keyes moved from Chinatown to the West Coast. There were rumors that Keyes had pissed off the wrong people in New York City (he owned huge sums of money to the local bookies), and the word was that Keyes either was told either "To Go West, Young Man, Go West," or go southbound six feet deep.

While on a modified lamsky in Los Angeles, Keyes took a gig as the boxing promoter at the East Side Arena, and as a sidelight, Keyes became a bodyguard for actress Mae West. There are no confirmed reports that West ever told Keyes to "Come up and see me sometime."

While in Hollywood, Keyes also took bit parts in several movies, including Hall Roach's "Captain Fury" (1939), which starred Victor McLaglen, Brian Aherne, and June Lang, who was married to Chicago mobster Johnny Roselli, a close pal of Johnny Keyes.

In 1942, Roselli was arrested, tried and convicted for extorting from Hollywood's elite, in addition to milking dry the International Alliance of Theatrical Stage Employees Union. As a result, the bad publicity caused by Roselli shenanigans flushed his wife, Lang's, movie career down the drain. As for Roselli, he came up wet himself, when in 1976 he was found dead in a 55-gallon drum floating in the waters off North Miami. The coroner put the cause of death as extreme lead poisoning.

In 1942, to avoid the L.A. heat caused by Roselli's actions, Johnny Keyes moved to San Diego, where he opened a restaurant called "Spaghetti Joe's," which is the nickname Damon Runyon gave Keyes while they bummed out together in New York City.

According to a Runyon syndicated newspaper column in July of 1943:

> *Johnny Keyes, the five-foot-three-inch former Mayor of Chinatown and now over 200 pounds, lost over $5,000 last night at the Del Mar Racetrack in San Diego. His only reply was, "Money don't mean nuthin' to me. It ain't your life. It ain't your wife. It's only money.'*

Over the years, Johnny Keyes was nothing if not consistent.

When Runyon wrote his famous play, *Guys and Dolls*, one of his degenerate-gambler characters, Harry the Horse, was based on my uncle, Johnny Keyes.

Runyon once said, "Johnny Keyes is Harry the Horse in the flesh."

On Monday, August 29, 1966, Johnny Keyes died in San Diego of a heart attack at the age of 74. Before he died, Keyes claimed he was still the Mayor of Chinatown in New York City, because no one in the last 42 years had challenged him for the office.

You can't make up stuff like this.

Snakeheads: Chinese Illegal Immigrant Smugglers - A Screenplay

By Joe Bruno

PUBLISHED BY:
Knickerbocker Literary Services

COVER BY:
Amazon Cover Creator

FADE IN:

EXT. CHINATOWN - NIGHT

The Chinese New Year's celebration is in full force.

Hordes of Chinese celebrants pack the sidewalks and the streets.

GONGS CLANG as a team of celebrants perform the CHINESE DRAGON DANCE in the street.

FIRECRACKERS EXPLODE at their feet.

BILLOWING SMOKE FILLS THE AIR.

CLOSE ON - CORNER STREET SIGN, which is written in both English and in Chinese:

"MOTT and BAYARD."

SUPERIMPOSE: CHINESE NEW YEAR 1996 - YEAR OF THE RAT.

INT. CHINATOWN TENEMENT APARTMENT - NIGHT

The SOUNDS of the CHINESE NEW YEAR'S CELEBRATION emanate from the street below.

A YOUNG CHINESE GIRL dressed only in a tattered knee-length smock sits barefoot on the floor. A chamber pot rests on the floor next to her.

She appears to be in her early teens, but because of her disheveled look she could several years older.

Her head is shaved; her thin legs are exposed, and her almond-shaped eyes scream fear.

Her hands are handcuffed behind her back, and a chain connected to the handcuffs is wrapped around a steam radiator.

We hear VOICES of men SPEAKING IN CHINESE in the hallway outside.

She wriggles her thin wrists behind her; desperately trying to slip through the handcuffs.

The CHINESE CHATTER outside the room stops.

We hear feet shuffle away from the door.

The door opens.

A middle-aged, CHUBBY CHINESE GANGSTER struts into the room. He's wearing a black leather jacket and a black shirt. Gold and diamond bling sparkle on his hands and around his neck. His jacket and shirt are open; exposing his Buddha-like belly. A saber-like KNIFE is stuffed into his belt.

He stops and stares at the young Chinese girl; his eyes sparkling with lust. He smiles, licks his lips; and then stalks towards the girl.

He removes his leather jacket and flings it on the floor.

She wriggles her boney wrists behind her. We see her thin right hand SLIP THROUGH THE CUFFS; then her left hand.

HER HANDS ARE NOW FREE.

                    CHINESE GANGSTER
      The rent is due now.
          (beat)
      You ready to pay?

He kneels down in front of her, removes the knife from under his belt and lays it on the floor next to him. He unzips his zipper, slides his pants down, and then tugs them off. He's now naked from the waist down.

He pulls her down onto her back and savagely tugs off her smock; leaving her completely naked.

With his hands, he roughly spreads her legs apart, leans over her, then mounts inside her.

They are face to face; her hands behind her, and her legs are scissored around his body.

He closes his eyes and MOANS IN PLEASURE as he slowly pulsates inside her.

She lays back and absorbs his thrusts; looking intermittently scared and disgusted.

He increases the speed of his movements; MOANING louder with every thrust.

She slowly slips her FREE RIGHT HAND from behind her.

Eyes still closed, he pumps her faster and faster; MOANING LOUDER AND LOUDER.

He achieves orgasm and then emits a PRIMAL SCREAM.

Exhausted, he collapses on top of her.

Quickly, she snatches the knife off the floor, and YELPING LIKE A MANIAC …

SHE STABS HIM REPEATEDLY IN THE BACK AND IN THE SIDE.

GRUNTING AND SCREAMING LOUDER WITH EVERY PLUNGE OF THE KNIFE.

His BLOOD SQUIRTS onto her face and into her mouth.

SHE SPITS HIS BLOOD BACK INTO HIS FACE.

She shoves him off her; turns him around, and straddles him. They are now face to face; with her on top.

She STABS him AGAIN, AGAIN, and AGAIN.

Her face is defiant. Low GROWLS, like from a beast in the wild, spew from her mouth.

SHE SCREAMS like a banshee as she ...

SLITS HIS THROAT FROM EAR TO EAR.

His BLOOD SQUIRTS upward; soaking her chest.

He rolls onto one side; then onto his back; his fat belly pointed toward the ceiling. His dead eyes are WIDE OPEN.

She puts on her smock and jumps to her feet. She stands, picks up his leather jacket, and drapes it around her shoulders.

Then, for good measure, she SPITS on his dead face.

She quietly opens the front door of the apartment and scans both ways down the hallway.

No one is in sight.

She scampers down the stairs; passing a few startled Chinese tenants; then sprints through the front door and out of the building.

EXT. CHINATOWN – NIGHT - CONTINUOUS

The young Chinese girl dashes out of the building and melts into the festive crowd.

We see her push past Chinese revelers, as she disappears into the night.

INT. WAREHOUSE - DAY

SUPERIMPOSE: PRESENT DAY

Three men in their late 20's unload a truck. They pile boxes of
HIGH DEFINITION DVD PLAYERS on the floor.

They are: PAULIE GRASSO, JIMMY RYAN, and BILLY THE
POLARK; three small-time wannabes with brains the size of
peas.

> PAULIE
> Marone, we must have close to 500 pieces here.

> JIMMY RYAN
> At $150 each, swag; we're looking at 75,000 clams. Nice
day's work.

> BILLY THE POLARK
> *(reading the printing on the DVD boxes)*
> Vafanculo! We're screwed.

> PAULIE
> What do you mean we're screwed?

> BILLY THE POLARK
> These are Toshiba HD DVD players ... Not Blue Rays.

> PAULIE
> What the fuck's the difference?

> BILLY THE POLARK
> The difference is that these players are obsolete.

> JIMMY RYAN
> What are you nuts? What's obsolete?

PAULIE
(To Billy the Polark)
You're obsolete.

BILLY THE POLARK
I'm telling you these players are worthless; like
Betamaxes were 25 years ago.

JIMMY RYAN
(confused)
What's a Betamax?

BILLY THE POLARK
Look ... these HD DVD players lost in a shootout with the
Blue Rays.

PAULIE
What's this baseball? Or hockey?
(beat)
Shootout ... Blue Rays ... I still think you're nuts.

BILLY THE POLARK
Listen ... there's two types of HD DVD players. Toshiba
HD DVD players and Sony Blue Ray HD DVD players.
The Sony's were better and cheaper, so Toshiba stopped
making HD DVD players.

PAULIE
So what? That makes the Toshibas we have more
valuable because there's less of them.
(beat)
The law of supply and demand.

BILLY THE POLARK
Except for one little problem. Neither player is
compatible with the other. And now all the HD DVD's are
made in the Blue Ray format.

PAULIE

So, you're telling me, we have 500 Toshiba HD DVD players and no movies to play on them.

BILLY THE POLARK
Yeah. That's basically what I'm tellin' you.

JIMMY RYAN
So, we're screwed.

BILLY THE POLARK
Basically.

PAULIE
Basically, I'd like to split your skull.

BILLY THE POLARK
Hey, don't kill the messenger. I'm just telling the truth here.

PAULIE
(brushes his hand though his hair)
My luck's been so bad lately, if it were raining tits, I'd get hit in the head with a flying cock.

JIMMY RYAN
Cock what? ... What cock? ...
(angry)
We ain't fags here.

PAULIE
Just start putting this shit back in the truck.
(beat)
Damn it! I need three Advil's and a stiff drink.

JIMMY RYAN
Now that you mention it, I got a load of hydrocodone I'm selling. How about a few dozen or so? I'll give you a good deal on them.

PAULIE
Just start loadin' the fuckin' truck.

The three wannabes start flinging the useless HD DVD players into the back of the open truck.

Life is tough, but it's tougher when you're stupid.

EXT. BROOKLYN RESIDENTIAL NEIGHBORHOOD - DAY

This beautiful tree-lined street is adorned with well-groomed one-and-two-story houses.

Sunshine galore. Birds are CHIRPING. All is right with the world.

INT. GRASSO RESIDENCE/DINING ROOM - DAY

Paulie, his sister LISA, and his father PETE are chowing down on pasta. While ...

Mother RITA places more dishes of ITALIAN FOOD on the table.

Paulie and Pete eat with like it's their last meal before they go to the electric chair. Lisa picks at her food like a bird.

> RITA
> *(Sits)*
> Ah. Finally.

> PAULIE
> I'd like to put a gun to Joe Girardi's head.

> RITA
> Joe the Butcher? ... What did he do to you?

> PETE
> No. Joe Girardi ... The manager of the New York Yankees.

> LISA
> *(picking at her food)*
> You guys and baseball ... Get a life.

                    PAULIE
Freakin' Yankees played like dogs all season long. And
now Detroit beats the crap out of them and the Yankees
are out of the playoffs ... See ya next year.

                    PETE
And Derek Jeter breaks his ankle too … Ain't' that a
bitch? … At his age he's lucky he plays next year.

                    PAULIE
Yeah Pop … Jeter is about your age ... Eighty somethin'.

                    PETE
Just eat and shut up.

JOHNNY GRASSO, the oldest child in the Grasso family,
saunters into the room. He's wearing an expensive Italian-cut
suit and striped tie.

Johnny takes off the suit jacket and hangs it on the back of his
chair. He's wearing a HOLSTERED GUN.

                    JOHNNY
          (sits)
Who's eighty-something?

                    PAULIE
Derek Jeter ... He's pop's age.

                    JOHNNY
          (picks up a fork)
Pop's still young enough to kick your fuckin' ass.

                    RITA
          (to Johnny)
Hey, no cursing at the kitchen table.

The three men attack their food with a vengeance.

RITA
(continuing; to Johnny)
And take off that gun. You know the rules. No guns at the kitchen table.

JOHNNY
(to Rita)
You made that rule for your son Paulie the crook. Not for your son Johnny the cop.
(eats)
I'm a decorated New York City Police Detective.

RITA
(points to Johnny's gun)
Lose the gun ... Right now!

JOHNNY
Okay, okay. Keep your shirt on, Mom.

Johnny stands from the table. He takes off the holstered gun, and places the gun and the holster on a nearby credenza, which is decorated with pictures of saints and a statue of the Virgin Mary.

A crucifix hangs on the wall behind the credenza. Above the crucifix, there's a picture of John F. Kennedy. Next to Kennedy's picture, is a picture of Frank Sinatra.

Johnny saunters back to the table. He sits, picks up a fork, and resumes shoveling food into his mouth.

PAULIE
(to Johnny)
Big brother, I have a nice present for you.

JOHNNY
(fork near his mouth)
For me? What?

PAULIE

I have DVD players for the entire family. The new ones that play high definition DVD's.

JOHNNY
(eating, not looking at Paulie)
Are they Toshibas?

PAULIE
Yeah. Toshibas.

JOHNNY
(fork in hand, he stares at Paulie)
They're paperweights.

PAULIE
Paperweights? ... No. They're high definition DVD players.

JOHNNY
Door stops.

PAULIE
Door stops?
(puts his hand up like a cop stopping traffic)
Stop!

JOHNNY
Listen ... Sony controls the high def DVD player market ... They call them Blue Rays.

RITA
Aren't the Blue Rays a baseball team?

JOHNNY
No, Ma. That's the Blue Jays.

PETE
The Blue Jays will have a better team than the Yankees

next year.

> **JOHNNY**
> *(shakes his head)*
> Getting back to Paulie's useless DVD players.
> *(to Paulie)*
> Throw them away. All the high def DVD's come in a Blue Ray format now. Those Toshibas are obsolete ... Like Betamaxes.

> **RITA**
> *(to Johnny)*
> Your father bought me a Betamax about 30 years ago ... I still use it to prop the door open in the attic.

> **PETE**
> How about we change the subject?

> **JOHNNY**
> Good idea. I just want to enjoy my food.

> **LISA**
> (To Johnny)
> Did you hear, they found another dead prostitute, this time in an alleyway on Crosby Street? I think that's number four ... Are you involved in that investigation?

> **JOHNNY**
> No. Homicide has that one. I'm working on the Chinese gang problem ... Besides, that's the first murder in the Fifth Precinct. The three other murders happened in different precincts uptown.

> **LISA**
> Yeah, that's scary. A girl can't walk the street these days.

> **PAULIE**
> *(to Lisa)*
> We're talking about hookers here, sis. A hard-working

girl like you has nothing to worry about.

LISA
Maybe. But it still gives me the creeps.

PETE
(To Johnny)
So, how's things in my old Little Italy neighborhood? …
Or should I say Chinatown?

JOHNNY
Same old, same old. The Italians are a dying breed in
Little Italy. The Chinese have basically taken over the
entire neighborhood. The dead bodies that do turn up;
they're all Chinese.

PAULIE
(makes the sign of the cross)
There is a God.

PETE
See? That's why we moved to Brooklyn in the first place.
The Chinks basically pushed us out of our own
neighborhood. Uncle Vito says he's up to his neck in
Chinks.

JOHNNY
Uncle Vito is also up to his neck in cash. The fact is, he
has an ongoing agreement with the Chinese Tong boss
Duk Tang.

PAULIE
You sure it's not Peking Duck?

JOHNNY
(shoots Paulie a dirty look)
Uncle Vito controls the Italian rackets and Duk Tang
controls the Chinese rackets. Every New Years, they
exchange fat envelopes as a show of good faith.

PAULIE
Uncle Vito should put a bomb in the next envelope he gives to that Chink.

JOHNNY
There's one thing Uncle Vito doesn't get a cut from.

PETE
What's that?

JOHNNY
The smuggling of illegal Chinese aliens from China. It's big business now; run by Chinese gangsters called Snakeheads.

RITA
(makes the sign of the cross)
What a horrible name - Snakeheads.

JOHNNY
There's Cantonese Snakeheads and then there's Fukienese Snakeheads. They don't even speak the same language, but they all work together ... All they care about is the money.

PETE
How does this operation work?

JOHNNY
The contacts are made in China. Poor Chinese Immigrants pay as much as 50 large to get smuggled into the United States. From China, they go from place to place by boat, and usually wind up somewhere in Canada. From there, they get smuggled into the United States, either in big vans, or sometimes even in the truck of cars

PAULIE
Marone ! 50 large? Those Chinks must be making a lotta

cabbage.

                    JOHNNY
More than you think. The Snakeheads sometimes even
use old fishing trawlers to smuggle the Chinese
immigrants in; fifty, a hundred, two hundred people at a
time. They stop a few miles off the coast of New York
City, and then are transferred to the mainland by small
boats.

                    PAULIE
There must be ways for us Italians to scarf down some of
that cavolo.

                    JOHNNY
Forget about it. It's a complete Chinese operation ... No
Lo Fon involved.

                    PAULIE
Screw those Chinks! They're stuffing Little Italy with
millions of those slanty-eyed bastards. They're making it
miserable for us Italians to live in our own neighborhood
... Some way they gotta fuckin' pay.

                    RITA
                 (to Paulie)
Hey, no cursing at the kitchen table.

                    PETE
                 (to Johnny)
So, how do you know so much about these Snakeheads?

                    JOHNNY
My partner Norman is Chinese. His parents were born in
China. He knows all about the Snakeheads, and how they
operate.

                    LISA

I think Norman is a snake too. But he's not bad-looking for an Asian.

PETE
(to Lisa)
Hey, I don't want no half-breeds in this family.

PAULIE
(to Johnny)
There must be a way for us to make some money off those Chinks.

JOHNNY
Yeah ... Sell them those fagese DVD players you wanted to stick us with.

PAULIE
Fuck you!

PETE, RITA, AND LISA
(in unison)
Hey, no cursing at the kitchen table!

EXT. ALLEY UNDER THE MANHATTAN BRIDGE NEAR THE EAST RIVER - NIGHT

Two CHINESE GANGSTERS rain punches and kicks on a fallen YOUNG CHINESE MALE.

CHINESE DRAGON MUSIC BLARES in the background.

FIRECRACKERS EXPLODE.

Chinese gangster Ah KAY, a boss in the Snakeheads, grabs the young Chinese male by the hair. He drags him to his knees.

> AH KAY
> Where's the rest of my money?

> YOUNG CHINESE MALE
> *(crying)*
> I pay ... I pay ... I pay 20 thousand dollars already ... I get the rest soon.

XIN LIN, Ah Kay's right-hand man, backhands the young Chinese male across the face.

> XIN LIN
> One week ... 30 thousand dollars ... Or we come back.

> YOUNG CHINESE MALE
> I try. I try.

Xin Lin lands a roundhouse right to young Chinese male's face. The young Chinese male falls flat on his back; blood oozes from his nose and mouth.

> XIN LIN
> Call China ... Call your relatives ... Tell them to pay our man in Guangzhou.

YOUNG CHINESE MALE
(sits up; wipes blood from his face with the back of his hand)
Okay, Okay. They pay ... Right away they pay.

AH KAY
They pay, or you die.

Ah Kay lands a savage KICK to the young Chinese male's face.

The young Chinese male spits teeth. More blood flows out both sides of his mouth, as he FALLS UNCONSCIOUS onto his back.

EXT. CHINATOWN - NIGHT

An unmarked police car negotiates traffic on Canal Street.

INT. UNMARKED POLICE CAR - NIGHT

Johnny Grasso is driving. His partner NORMAN WONG sits next to him.

SINATRA is SINGING on the car radio. Norman is SINGING along with Sinatra.

Norman's English is impeccable. There's no trace of a Chinese accent.

                    NORMAN
        Ah, what I'd give to be Italian ... The food; the songs; the
women ... Your sister Lisa...

                    JOHNNY
        Forget about my sister Lisa.

                    NORMAN
        What do you mean? The girl's obviously crazy about me.

                    JOHNNY
        Yeah, she's crazy alright. But my father's crazier. And
he's got a gun.

                    NORMAN
        I don't plan on dating your father.

Johnny shoots Norman the evil eye; then changes the subject

                    JOHNNY
        Looks like another dead hooker showed up last night ...
        This one they found in our precinct on Crosby Street.

NORMAN
So what? ...That's one less whore the city has to worry about.

JOHNNY
You always were a sensitive guy.

Norman pulls out his wallet. He removes a snapshot of a beautiful Chinese girl, and hands the snapshot to Johnny.

NORMAN
Now this is a real woman; not like the ones turning up dead.

JOHNNY
(looks at snapshot)
Nice looking chick. Is this your sister?

NORMAN
No, my sister's so ugly she'd break the camera. This is my friend Ping. She's a businesswoman in Chinatown.

JOHNNY
So why do you keep a businesswoman's picture in your wallet?

NORMAN
To impress jerkoffs like you.

JOHNNY
Scumbag.

NORMAN
(puts picture back into his wallet)
How about we cut a deal? ... A double date ... Me and your sister, Lisa ... You and Ping.

JOHNNY

A double date?

NORMAN
Sure. What have you got to lose?

JOHNNY
(*repeats*)
What have I got to lose?
(*beat*)
My balls. That's what I've got to lose. If my father finds out I set up my sister with a Chinaman, he'd cut off my balls.

NORMAN
This is a gorgeous Chinese girl I'm dangling in front of your face.

JOHNNY
(*thinking*)
Ok. You've got a deal. But I'll deliver my sister to this date. If my old man finds out about you and her, he'll have a shit fit.

NORMAN
(*singing with Sinatra*)
I'VE GOT THE WORLD ON A STING, SITTING ON A RAINBOW! .... GOT THAT STRING AROUND MY FINGER! ...

JOHNNY
(*singing*)
WHAT A WORLD! ... WHAT A LIFE! ...

NORMAN
(*singing*)
I'M IN LOVE.

EXT. CHINATOWN – NIGHT - CONTINUOUS

The unmarked police car weaves through Chinatown traffic.
The car's police lights are FLASHING and the siren BLARING;
for no particular reason except that Norman figures he's a cop
and can do whatever he wants.

EXT. ATLANTIC OCEAN - LATE NIGHT

New York City's lights illuminate the background.

EXT. A FISHING TRAWLER - LATE NIGHT

The FISHING TRAWLER rocks back and forth in a FURIOUS
RAINSTORM.

A SMALL ROWBOAT bobs violently next to the trawler. A
disheveled CHINESE MAN sits in the row boat. He has an oar in
the water on each side of the rowboat, which looks like it might
capsize any second.

Ah Kay stands on the deck of the trawler. Xin Lin stands next to
him.

TWO CHINESE GANGSTERS drag three CHINESE MALE
PRISONERS onto the deck of the trawler.

Ah Kay motions to the man in the rowboat to move the rowboat
closer to the trawler.

Xin Lin grabs one prisoner.

> XIN LIN
> *(in Chinese)*
> Jump! ... Now!

The man hesitates, then jumps into the rowboat.

Ah Kay grabs the second prisoner.

> **AH KAY**
> *(in Chinese)*
> You too! … Jump!

The second prisoner jumps down into the rowboat.

Xin Lin grabs the third prisoner.

> **XIN LIN**
> *(in Chinese)*
> Now you! ... Jump!

The third prisoner jumps. He mistimes his leap, and FALLS INTO THE RAGING WATERS.

The three men in the rowboat try to save the drowning man, but they are too weak to drag him into the rowboat.

The drowning man struggles to swim. A man in the rowboat offers the drowning man an OAR. The drowning man grabs the oar.

A wave crashes into the drowning man, and he falls back into the water; losing the oar in the process.

The rowboat tips and almost capsizes. The three men in the rowboat SCREAM.

A GUNSHOT BLASTS from the trawler.

The drowning man takes a BULLET IN THE CHEST and drowns.

Holding a smoking gun, Ah Kay looks down at the rowboat.

> **AH KAY**

(in Chinese; to the men in the boat)
Row to shore! ... Now!

The original man in the rowboat hands oars to the other three.
They row away into the darkness.

                    AH KAY
          (continuing; in English to Xin Lin)
That's part of the cost of doing business, bro.

                    XIN LIN
Yeah, but what a waste of a bullet.
          (beat)
And what about the money we lose for the creep we just
killed? ... We were supposed to smuggle him into the
United States?

                    AH KAY
          (smiles)
We already got twenty grand from his family in China ...
We'll collect the rest.

                    XIN LIN
How? ... The guy's dead.

                    AH KAY
We'll collect the money before they realize he's dead.

                    XIN LIN
Suppose they find out he's dead before we get our
money?

                    AH KAY
Then we'll just kill one family member at a time until we
get our money ... Believe me, after we kill one; the others
will pay.
          (spits into the ocean)
That's the best part of being a gangster.

Both Chinese gangsters LAUGH like hyenas.

EXT. FORLINIS RESTAURANT - NIGHT

The lit restaurant canopy sparkles "FORLINIS."

Jolly patrons enter and the exit the bustling restaurant.

INT. FORLINIS RESTAURANT – NIGHT

Red leather booths line the perimeter and several tables lie in the center of the room. All the seats are taken.

Gold-framed portraits decorate the walls.

The portraits depict:

"An old man smiling."

"A young woman singing."

"A man playing a violin."

The male patrons in Forlini's dining room wear sports jackets and suits. They are obviously professional men; not gangsters.

The women are decked out in expensive suits, dresses, and skirts. Their diamond rings and necklaces sparkle. Classy chicks; no "Mob Wives" here.

There's a happy CHATTER in the background.

Johnny and Norman sit on one side of a corner booth. Lisa and PING sit facing them.

Her jet black hair falls down Ping's back to her waist. She is wearing her trademark black-framed CHRISTIAN DIOR GLASSES.

Dinner is done and the waiter puts the check on the table.

The owner, DEREK FORLINI, arrives at the table.

> ### DEREK
> Can I buy you people an after-dinner drink?

> ### JOHNNY
> Absolutely ... Make it four doubles of your finest.

NORMAN picks up the check and scans it.

> ### NORMAN
> *(to Derek)*
> I know all about inflation ... But your prices look like telephone numbers.

> ### DEREK
> Only if your eyes are slanted.

> ### NORMAN
> *(hands Derek a credit card)*
> Ok .... I'll let you extort me; just this one time.

> ### DEREK
> I'll be back with the drinks. All Sambucas?

> ### LISA
> Yes. Sambuca.

> ### PING
> I'll take a Sambuca too.

> ### JOHNNY
> Make mine a black Sambuca.

> ### NORMAN
> Two Black Bucas.

DEREK
Two regular Sambucas for the lovely ladies ... Two Black Bucas for the bad guys.

JOHNNY
(to Derek)
Tell your story walking.

Derek smirks, then exits the dining room.

LISA
Boy, you guys are a tough audience.

JOHNNY
(to Ping)
So Norman tells me you own a travel agency in Chinatown.

PING
I do.

NORMAN
That's how I met Ping; arranging a trip to China to see my family.

JOHNNY
(to Ping)
Well, maybe I can use you in the future.

PING
(smiles)
I hope you're talking about my travel agency.

JOHNNY
(grins)
What else would I be talking about?

PING
(to Johnny)

Tell me about your job ... Any interesting cases lately?

                    JOHNNY
To be quite honest, the Fifth Precinct doesn't have much
crime, except for organized crime; both Italian and
Chinese organized crime.

                    PING
Well, that should keep you busy.

                    JOHNNY
Sort of ... But the problem is the Chinese people
traditionally won't report crimes to the New York City
Police Department. They won't even talk to Chinese-
American police officers like Norman.

                    NORMAN
That's right. A few years back, a Chinese store owner on
Canal Street filled a police report complaining about
being shaken down by the Vietnamese Born to Kill Gang.
Before we could do anything about it, he was shot and
killed right in front of his family; in his own store, no less.

                    PING
I remember that.

                    JOHNNY
Since then, the Chinese store owners won't complain to us
about anything ... The gangs scared them away.

Derek arrives at the table with a tray of drinks.

                    NORMAN
Look who's here ... Artie Bucco.

                    LISA
Who's Artie Bucco?
        (beat)
You mean Osso Bucco?

NORMAN
You know, Artie Bucco; from the Sopranos.

LISA
I don't like the opera.

DEREK
(distributes the drinks)
Two double Bucas ... Two double black Bucas.
(to Johnny)
Anything else?

JOHNNY
Yes, the lovely sight of you leaving our table.

DEREK
(smiles)
Enjoy.

Derek exits the dining room.

LISA
(to Johnny)
Tell Ping about the Snakeheads.

JOHNNY
No, she doesn't want to hear about that garbage.

PING
But I do. Tell me. Please.

JOHNNY
Norman's more the expert about them than I am.

NORMAN
Well, since you asked.
(beat)
These disgraziata Snakeheads...

JOHNNY
(disgusted)
Disgraziata? ...
(to Ping)
Norman thinks he's Italian.

NORMAN
Okay. Okay. These ... Snakeheads ... smuggle illegal
Chinese immigrants into this country. Then they torture
them if they don't pay the $50,000 fee on time.

LISA
Yeah, but why do they call them Snakeheads?

NORMAN
Because, as legend has it, when the illegal immigrants
sneak through the fences, they look like little snakes from
the distance.

LISA
That's stupid.

JOHNNY
And so is this conversation ... What do you say we split?

PING
No. Tell me more about the Snakeheads. I'm interested.

JOHNNY
What's to tell? ... The Fujianese gangs used to control all
the Snakehead trade. Now we have the Cantonese Big
Circle Boys to contend with.

LISA
(concerned)
Big Circle Boys?

NORMAN

Yeah … that's what they call themselves. If you ask me, they're the Big "Circle Jerk" Boys.

> PING
> *(shakes her head)*
> Both Norman and I are Cantonese. He should know the Big Circle Boys are no joke … They're dangerous people.

> JOHNNY
> *(standing)*
> You guys ready? My father has a stop watch on my sister, Lisa.

> LISA
> Don't listen to him. My father's asleep already.

> JOHNNY
> Yeah, he's asleep … With a gun in his lap.

> NORMAN
> *(standing)*
> I don't want no trouble.

> PING
> *(standing; to Lisa)*
> Ready?

> LISA
> *(standing)*
> Ok. Let's blow this popsicle stand.

The two couples exit the dining room.

EXT. FORLINI'S RESTAURANT – NIGHT - CONTINUOUS

The four people stroll into the parking lot next door.

> NORMAN
> I'll drive Lisa home to Brooklyn

JOHNNY
Ok ... But remember my father ... Be smart ... Don't drop my sister off in front of our house.

Norman hands the parking stub to the CHINESE PARKING ATTENDANT. The attendant looks at the back of the stub and hands Norman the keys to this car.

NORMAN
(to attendant)
How much I owe you?

PARKING ATTENDANT
Nothing ... The Forlinis took care of it for you already.

LISA
(to Norman)
And you're always breaking their balls.

NORMAN
The Forlinis are good people ... I've always said that.

Norman opens the front passenger door for Lisa.

Lisa kisses Johnny's cheek.

JOHNNY
(to Lisa)
Go straight home ... Don't let Norman get cute with you.

LISA
Norman get cute? ... I'll break his nose.

Lisa slides inside the front passenger seat of the car.

NORMAN
Tough chick ... I like them tough.

Norman struts around the front of the car. He opens the driver's door and gets behind the wheel.

JOHNNY
(to Norman)
Remember, take my sister straight home. No gallivanting ... My father's a nut.

LISA
(from inside the car; to Norman)
Don't listen to my brother. My father's a pussy cat.

JOHNNY
Yeah, a Bengal tiger pussycat.

Norman puts the car in gear and exits the parking lot.

JOHNNY
(continuing; to Ping)
I'll walk you home ... 50 Bayard Street ... Right?

PING
How did you know where I live?

JOHNNY
(puts his arm around her shoulder)
I'm a cop ... I know everything.

EXT. BAYARD STREET - NIGHT

Johnny and Ping stop in front of 50 BAYARD STREET, a luxurious high-rise apartment building, set in the midst of 100-year-old tenements.

THE MANHATTAN BRIDGE sparkles in the background.

> PING
> Would you like to come up for a night cap?

> JOHNNY
> That night cap sounds great ... But I have an early day tomorrow ... Can I get a rain check?

> PING
> Why, of course.

> JOHNNY
> No expiration date?

> PING
> (smiling)
> Within reason.

> JOHNNY
> I'll take the rain check ... You fill in the expiration date.

Johnny extends his right hand; expecting a handshake.

Ping takes his hand. She kisses Johnny on both cheeks, just like the neighborhood Italians do.

> PING
> (smiles)
> Call me.

JOHNNY
I don't know ... When someone kisses an Italian on both cheeks, something bad usually happens.

PING
Not if a Chinese girl does the kissing.

JOHNNY
I'll take your word for it.

PING
(waves)
Toodles.

Ping turns and strolls into her building.

JOHNNY
(ogles her as she enters the building)
Madone!

Johnny saunters towards the Manhattan Bridge.

EXT. DESOLATE BROOKLYN STREET - NIGHT

Norman's unmarked police car is parked. The windows are fogged, like something hot and heavy is going on inside.

INT. UNMARKED CAR - NIGHT

Norman and Lisa are kissing in the back seat of the car.

Norman tries to unbutton Lisa's blouse. She slaps his hands away.

> NORMAN
> I guess I got a little carried away.

> LISA
> *(annoyed)*
> If you keep that up, you will get carried away.

> NORMAN
> Okay. My bad ... It won't happen again.

> LISA
> *(angry)*
> You're damn right, it won't happen again.

Lisa pushes open the back door of the car.

> NORMAN
> Where are you going?

> LISA
> I'm walking home ... It's only a couple of blocks.
> *(beat)*
> Johnny is right about my father. He's not exactly in love with the Chinese.

Lisa exits the car.

EXT. DESOLATE BROOKLYN STREET – NIGHT - CONTINUOUS

Lisa struts quickly down the block. Her high heels are CLICKING on the sidewalk.

Norman follows her in his car. He pulls the car alongside her.

> NORMAN
> *(from inside the car)*
> Come on. Get in. I'll drive you home.

> LISA
> *(annoyed)*
> Not a chance in hell.

Lisa keeps walking, faster and faster, without looking back at the car.

> NORMAN
> Okay ... Goodnight.

Lisa's face screams anger. She shoots Norman the Italian Salute, then she breaks into a jog and disappears around the corner.

INT. UNMARKED CAR – NIGHT - CONTINUOUS

Norman's face is contorted with rage. He grips the steering wheel, as if he wants to turn it into sawdust.

> Norman
> Fuckin' Guinea bitch!

EXT. ITALIAN SOCIAL CLUB - DAY

The social club's windows are painted black. Several goombahs mill around outside; whispering in each other's ears; like English spies in Nazi Germany.

In the doorway next door, four middle-aged men HARMONIZE a do wop song.

INT. ITALIAN SOCIAL CLUB - DAY

Wooden tables and chairs dot the floors. An espresso machine sits on top of a small bar.

Photos decorate all four walls.

The pictures consist of:

"Italian boxers."

"Italian singers."

"Pope Pius XII."

"Sophia Loren wearing a loincloth."

Frank Sinatra croons a song on the jukebox.

Paulie sits at a corner table, across from CARLO LANDANO, a made-man in the neighborhood Italian-American crime family. Both men are picking from a plate of Italian cheeses and Italian cold cuts.

> CARLO
> Those fuckin' Patriots destroyed you. Your weekly tab is up to 50 thousand clams. What are we gonna do here?

PAULIE

Brady gets hurt and is out for the fuckin' year. I got no fuckin' luck.

CARLO

Where you come off betting dimes anyway? That's way over your head. I would never have approved it if it weren't for your Uncle Vito.

PAULIE

I don't know ... I guess I just got carried away.

CARLO

If you don't pay your tab on time, you will get carried away.

PAULIE

Don't worry ... I'm good for it.

CARLO
(eats)
Look, I'll do you a favor. I'll front you the fifty grand. At two points a week, instead of the usual three; as a favor to your Uncle Vito.

PAULIE

Thanks ... I consider it an honor.

CARLO

But no more dimes on a game ... Two hundred clams ... Tops.

PAULIE

Done.

CARLO
(sticks his forefinger under Paulie's nose)
And don't go bettin' with any other books. That will definitely get my attention, and I will not be happy.

                    PAULIE
        Jeez ... How can a man get even betting only 200 bucks a
game?

                    CARLO
        Be a man. Go out and steal for a living. Do a score ... like
every other man in this "thing of ours."

                    PAULIE
        I'm not even officially in this "thing of ours." I'm still
making my bones.

                    CARLO
        Keep up your stupid gamblin' and you'll be bones in a
fuckin' coffin.

                    PAULIE
        Speaking of scores ... I've got this great idea. It involves
shaking down the Chinks ... It could be a big
moneymaker for us.

                    CARLO
        Big moneymaker?
                    (eats)
        Talk to me. I'm all ears.

EXT. CHINESE COFFEE SHOP - NIGHT

Two CHINESE GANG MEMBERS stand by the front door like sentinels. They have sneers on their faces; like they'd like to bite the heads off rattlesnakes.

INT. CHINESE COFFEE SHOP - NIGHT

Carlo and Tong leader DUK TANG sit at a table. Both men are sipping brandy from a snifter.

Paulie and Ah Kay sit at a table next to them; playing bodyguard for their bosses. Each stares darts at the other, hoping the other blinks first.

>   CARLO
>   I tell you, Duk, this is a damn good brandy.

>   DUK
>   Actually, my friend, it's Cognac ... Louie XIII ... A gift
> from your Don Vito last New Years.

>   CARLO
>   Right ... Cognac.
>   (sips; smacks lips)
>   You know, we've had a wonderful relationship ... the
>   Chinese and the Italians in Chinatown ... For over 100
>   years now.

>   DUK
>   Yes, my dear friend. All the Mayors of Chinatown have
>   maintained strong relationships with our Italian
>   colleagues ... Mock Duck in the early 1900's ... Uncle
>   Seven ... the honorable Benny Ong ... Man Bun Lee ...
>   And myself ... Ours were, and still are very strong and
>   profitable relationships indeed.

CARLO

And every New Year's we exchange envelopes as a show
of good faith and prosperity.

DUK

Yes ... good faith and prosperity.

CARLO

We each handle our own people's needs, but share in the
profits.
          (beat)
To a certain extent, I mean.

DUK
          (wary)
My friend, I sense some reticence in your voice.

CARLO

Well, there is this situation with your smuggling of illegal
Chinese immigrants into Chinatown. You haven't let us
wet our beaks, not even a little bit, in this huge
moneymaking operation of yours.

DUK
          (puts his glass on the table)
What does that have to do with the Italians?
          (beat)
Now, if the situation were reversed, and it were you
smuggling in your own people, we would not expect a
share of your profits.

CARLO

Well that's one way to look at it. But the way we see it is
this.
          (beat)
You've been smuggling in thousands, maybe tens of
thousands of illegal Chinese every year; crowding our
streets so bad you can't walk two feet without bumping
into a Chinaman ... These are the same streets we both

share to do our business.

                    DUK
So, the streets are a little more crowded. How is that an
issue?

                    CARLO
It's not just that. It's these stupid shootings ... Chinese
gangsters charging into restaurants ... shooting up the
joints like maniacs. White people are afraid to come into
Chinatown.
          (beat)
Bottom line. That's bad for all our businesses.

                    DUK
Oh, I hardly think that's the case.

                    CARLO
Look at it this way ... We have only a handful of Italians
still living in Little Italy. You have millions of Chinese in
our streets, and more coming in very day. They feed your
bellies, but not ours.
          (beat)
When's the last time you saw Chinese people eating in an
Italian restaurant?
          (beat)
Like how about never?

                    DUK
You are right about that ... But you must understand
your Italian food is far too rich for our tastes ... and so
fattening too.

                    CARLO
So, because your millions of Chinese here in our
neighborhood don't feed us a penny, we need the white
tourists to make our businesses prosper. Your crazy
Chinese gangs are chasing them away ... Nobody in their
right mind wants to get a belly full of lead with their

lasagna.

                    DUK
And this is coming from our friend, Don Vito?

                    CARLO
Of course it is. I wouldn't discuss somethin' like this
without the okay from my boss.

                    DUK
My first indication is to say no.
          (beat)
But let me think it through and I will get back to you.

                    CARLO
How long will this take?

                    DUK
Maybe a few days ... A few weeks ...Who knows? ... I was
not expecting this.

Duk and Carlo stand at the same time. They shake hands, but
they are not smiling.

                    CARLO
          (to Paulie)
Come on. Let's go.

Paulie stands. He shoots Ah Kay a stare, like he'd like to
strangle the Chinese bastard.

Paulie saunters towards the front door. He stops; turns around.

                    PAULIE
          (to Ah Kay)
Be seeing you around, pal.

                    AH KAY
          (smirks)

Any time.

Carlo and Paulie exit the coffee shop.

> DUK
> *(to Ah Kay)*
> That was not a conversation I expected ... And I did not appreciate Carlo's attitude.

> AH KAY
> Me neither ... What do you propose we do?

> DUK
> Nothing. Absolutely nothing. We'll just wait.
> *(beat)*
> When the time is right, we will make the first move. The Chinese outnumber the Italians ten to one in this neighborhood. They would be foolish to engage us in a war they cannot possibly win.

Duk and Ah Kay take a seat at Duk's table. Duk pours them each a shot of cognac. They both down the cognac in one huge gulp.

> AH KAY
> *(slaps glass on the table)*
> Fuck those greaseball bastards!

EXT. CHINESE COFFEE SHOP - NIGHT

Carlo and Paulie exit the coffee shop.

They push their way past the two Chinese guards. They hurry down the street and stop at a parked black Lincoln Town Car.

> CARLO
> *(looks back over his shoulder at the Chinese coffee shop)*
> That did not go the way I expected.

PAULIE
So what's our next move?

CARLO
It might be time for us to land a sucker punch.
(runs his hand through his hair)
A huge sucker punch ... From way out in left field

Paulie opens the front passenger door for Carlo and Carlo slides into the front passenger seat.

Paulie walks around front of car, and opens the driver's door. He gets behind the wheel.

The Lincoln darts out of the parking spot. BURNING RUBBER.

We see the two Chinese bodyguards smirk, then hit each other with a LOUD SMACKING high five.

EXT. CANAL STREET - DAWN

A slice of light is visible on the HORIZON.

THREE CHINESE GANG MEMBERS are driving in a Hummer towards the Holland Tunnel.

Rap music BLARES from their car radio.

There is light car traffic and no pedestrians are in sight.

A black sedan, looking like an unmarked police car, screeches out from a side street. It CRASHES INTO THE HUMMER.

THREE MEN with stockings over their faces, sprint from the unmarked sedan.

TWO MEN FIRE HANDGUNS. THE THIRD FIRES A MACHINE GUN.

Heavy gunfire BLASTS into the Hummer.

THE HUMMER'S WINDOWS SHATTER.

BULLETS RIDDLE THE HUMMER'S DOORS, ROOF, AND HOOD.

The Chinese gang members inside the Hummer flinch violently; like puppets with their strings being yanked one way, then another.

One at a time, the three Chinese gang members stop flinching; until all three have keeled over dead.

The three gunmen sprint toward A WAITING CAR. They pile inside.

The car speeds away.

INT. INSIDE OF GETAWAY CAR - CONTINUOUS

The three shooters remove the stockings from their heads and the gloves from their hands.

We see they are Paulie, Billy the Polark, and Jimmy Ryan.

Carlo is the getaway driver.

> CARLO
> Good work boys ... Now let's go eat.

> PAULIE
> The Market Diner?

> CARLO
> The Market Diner closed for good last year ... I know a nice joint on Ninth Avenue.

> PAULIE
> How about that diner in Jersey?

> CARLO
> *(Annoyed)*
> What are you nuts? ... There's cameras in the Holland Tunnel.

> JIMMY RYAN
> I want a big fat cheeseburger.

> BILLY THE POLARK
> No burgers ... I've got to have ketchup on my burgers. I've seen enough red for   tonight.

> CARLO
> Fuck 'em. We're going to Wo Hop on Mott Street ... right in the heart of Chinatown. It's been open 24 hours a day

for the past hundred fuckin' years.

PAULIE

Yeah. Fuck 'em ... It's still our neighborhood.

CARLO

You're fuckin' right it is ... We're going to Wo Hop and we ain't paying a fuckin' cent either ... I'll just put it on my tab.

PAULIE

You have a tab at Wo Hop?

CARLO

(smiles)

I do now.

EXT. CANAL STREET – EARLY MORNING

The sun is up and traffic is starting to build. Pedestrians are hustling to work.

The BULLET-RIDDLED HUMMER and the UNMARKED CAR are roped off in a crime scene.

THREE SETS OF PARAMEDICS carry THREE SHEET-COVERED BODIES. The paramedics put the sheet-covered bodies in THREE SEPARATE AMBULANCES.

Johnny and Norman flash their badges to a cop guarding the crime scene.

They step under the yellow crime scene tape and approach a uniformed policeman.

>   JOHNNY
>   *(to policeman)*
>   You the first on the scene?

>   POLICEMAN
>   Yes, sir.

>   JOHNNY
>   I'm Detective Grasso.
>   *(nods toward Norman)*
>   This is my partner Detective Wong ... What do you have
> for us?

>   POLICEMAN
>   Three dead Chinese gang members ... Shot dead in the
> Hummer.

>   NORMAN
>   How do you know they were gang members?

POLICEMAN
They all had guns in their possession. But they were killed before they could draw their weapons.

JOHNNY
And the other car?

POLICEMAN
Could be an accident. But I don't think so.

NORMAN
Anything else?

POLICEMAN
Yeah. The dead men had a combined ten thousand dollars in cash on them ... Give or take a few bucks ... And a large stash of drugs too.

NORMAN
Make sure all the cash and drugs are vouchered properly. Capice?

POLICEMAN
Absolutely.

NORMAN
(sarcastic)
Yeah right.

JOHNNY
(to policeman)
Were there any witnesses?

POLICEMAN
There was an old Chinese woman coming out of the subway. She said she saw three masked men jump into a waiting car. She said she thought they were white ... But this woman is as old as dirt and not a very reliable

witness.

                    JOHNNY
          Thanks ... Keep us posted.

                    POLICEMAN
          Will do, Detective Grasso.

                    NORMAN
               (to policeman)
          Remember, voucher all the money and the drugs. I'll be
checking up on you.

The policeman stares at Norman. SEETHING.

Johnny and Norman walk back to their unmarked car.

                    JOHNNY
          That wasn't nice what you said to that cop ... He's one of
us.

                    NORMAN
          Fuck him.
               (beat)
          Hey, maybe it was just a case of drug-induced road rage.
Case closed.

                    JOHNNY
          What about the witness?

                    NORMAN
          Old Chinese woman ... Probably half blind ... Can't say
her statement is too reliable.

                    JOHNNY
          I hope you're right. What we don't need now is a race war
in Chinatown.

                    NORMAN

That would not be good.

                    JOHNNY
You look a little under the weather.

                    NORMAN
Couldn't sleep last night. Upset stomach. Must have been
something I ate at Forlinis.

                    JOHNNY
Forlinis' food was fine. You must have a stomach virus,
or something.

                    NORMAN
Yeah, maybe.

                    JOHNNY
You hungry now?

                    NORMAN
Yeah. Let's go get some Chinese breakfast ... Some dim
sum ... There's a great joint on Pell Street.

                    JOHNNY
Okay. But no Chinese chicken feet. Just the sight of them
makes me sick.

                    NORMAN
How about some cha siu bao?

                    JOHNNY
Steamed or baked?

                    NORMAN
The steamed taste mushy ... Let's go for the baked.

                    JOHNNY
Ten-four.

The two detectives get into their unmarked car; Norman at the wheel. He makes a U-turn and heads back towards Chinatown.

INT. ITALIAN SOCIAL CLUB - DAY

Paulie struts through the front door.

Dean Martin is crooning on the juke box.

Several meaty thugs stand at the bar, sipping espresso. Other hoods sit at two tables, playing cards. Two of them wear 1940's-type fedoras on their fat heads.

One of the hoods wearing hats is PHILLY GUNS; the boss Vito's bodyguard.

> PAULIE
> *(to Philly Guns)*
> How's it going, Philly?

> PHILLY GUNS
> *(puts down his cards)*
> Doing good.
> *(nods towards the back room)*
> Carlo's in the back.

Paulie knocks at a door marked private.

> CARLO'S VOICE (O.S.)

> The door's open.

INT. ITALIAN SOCIAL CLUB/BACK ROOM - CONTINUOUS

Paulie enters the back room.

Carlo sits at a small round table. He's sipping espresso and scanning the sports pages in the New York Post.

                         CARLO
          Close the door behind you … And lock it.

Paulie closes and locks the door.

                         PAULIE
             What's up?

                         CARLO
                  (points to a chair opposite him)
             Have a seat.

A BOOMBOX sits on Carlo's table. Carlo turns it on and pumps
up the volume. AC/DC BLARES from the boombox. The music
is DEAFENING.

                         PAULIE
                  (hands over his ears)
          Whoa!

                         CARLO
                  (softly)
             The walls have ears.

Paulie takes a seat opposite Carlo. He hands Carlo an envelope.

Both men lean across the table; their noses almost touching.

                         PAULIE
             First week's vig.

                         CARLO
             Don't forget to keep it coming every week.

                         PAULIE
             No problem ... I have a few things in the works.

                         CARLO
             Let me remind you, any money you kick up to me from a

score is not a vig payment. Both are separate obligations.

                    PAULIE
Of course ... I'm not stupid.

                    CARLO
Anyone who says they are not stupid ... They're usually
stupid.

                    PAULIE
Whatever.

                    CARLO
          (makes a shooting motion with his thumb and
    forefinger)
Did you lose those things?

                    PAULIE
Dead and buried.

                    CARLO
I heard there was a witness ... Some old Chinese lady
coming out of the subway.

                    PAULIE
So what? Slantly eyes have trouble seeing ... Especially
old, slantly eyes.

                    CARLO
Yeah, you're probably right ... But who the fuck knows
what people are thinkin'?

                    PAULIE
Thinkin' and knowin' are two different things.

                    CARLO
Not in this "thing of ours."

We hear a BIG EXPLOSION FROM THE FRONT ROOM.

Paulie and Carlo dive under the table.

THE ROOM IS FILLED WITH SMOKE.

SCREAMS emanate from the front room.

Paulie slowly opens the door leading to the front room.

INT. ITALIAN SOCIAL CLUB/FRONT ROOM - CONTINUOUS

FIRE FLICKERS THROUGHOUT THE ROOM, and...

HEAVY SMOKE BILLOWS THROUGHOUT THE ROOM.

TABLES AND CHAIRS ARE DESTROYED.

Several mobsters LAY MOANING on the floor. Many of them are bleeding from head wounds.

Philly Guns tries to stand, but he falls flat on his face.

> CARLO
> *(grabs Paulie's arm)*
> Quick. Out the back door.

> PAULIE
> We gotta help Philly Guns

Carlo pulls Paulie into the back room.

INT. ITALIAN SOCIAL CLUB/BACK ROOM - CONTINUOUS

> PAULIE
> What about Philly Guns?

> CARLO

Fuck Philly Guns ... I owe him twenty grand ... If he croaks, my debt is erased from the books.

                    PAULIE
But Philly Guns is still alive ... And he's a made guy.

                    CARLO
(opens the back door leading to the backyard)
Worry about yourself.
(pulls Paulie towards the open door)
Now let's go!

Carlo pushes Paulie out the back door. Then he follows Paulie out the door.

EXT. ITALIAN SOCIAL CLUB/BACK YARD - CONTINUOUS

Paulie and Carlo dash down a narrow alley. They jump over a fence. Then sprint through the back door of an adjourning tenement building.

INT. TENEMENT BUILDING - CONTINUOUS

Not being in the best of shape, Carlo and Paulie stumble through the decrepit building and stagger out the front door.

EXT. LITTLE ITALY STREET - CONTINUOUS

Carlo and Paulie exit the building. They stare down the street towards the Italian social club.

The Italian social club's storefront is ABLAZE.

HUGE CLOUDS OF SMOKE obscure our view of the storefront.

FIRE ENGINES BLARE IN THE BACKGROUND.

Carlo and Paulie dash to a parked LINCOLN TOWN CAR.
They jump in and Carlo gets behind the wheel.

Carlo quickly backs up the Lincoln; SCREECHING back to the
corner.

Carlo shifts the car into drive. The Lincoln BURNS RUBBER
around the corner and disappears.

EXT. CHINATOWN TRAVEL AGENCY - DAY

Johnny strolls into the travel agency.

INT. CHINATOWN TRAVEL AGENCY - CONTINUOUS

Ping is doing paperwork at her desk.

Johnny enters.

> ### JOHNNY
> Have lunch yet?

> ### PING
> *(bright smile)*
> No. Not yet.

> ### JOHNNY
> I'm buying.

> ### PING
> Sounds like a plan.

> ### JOHNNY
> Chinese food okay with you.

> ### PING
> *(puts on her coat)*
> No. I only eat Italian food ... Meatball egg foo young.
> *(kisses his cheek)*
> But I have to make a stop first.

Johnny extends his arm and Lisa takes it. They strut through the front door like they don't have a care in the world.

INT. CHINESE SOUP KITCHEN - DAY

SEVERAL CHINESE WOMEN stand in line. Waiting for...

Food distributed by TWO CHINESE MEN standing behind a long lunchroom counter.

Chinese chatter REVERBERATES thought the room.

Ping leads Johnny past the counter to a door marked private. She knocks on the door.

> MAN'S VOICE (O.S.)
>
> Come in.

INT. CHINESE SOUP KITCHEN/OFFICE - CONTINUOUS

An elderly Chinese man named HOUSIE greets them at the door.

> HOUSIE
> *(to Ping)*
> How come you not spooning out food behind the counter?

> PING
> I have a date for lunch ... Housie, meet Detective Johnny Grasso. From the 5th Precinct.

> JOHNNY
> *(shakes Housie's hand)*
> My pleasure, Housie.

> HOUSIE
> *(bows)*
> Venerable New York city policeman ... I am very honored.

Ping hands Housie an envelope.

Housie takes the envelope and peeks inside.

HOUSIE

Sister Ping, you are so kind ... I see your travel agency business is doing very well.

PING

Just like in the Sanitation Department ... Business is picking up.

HOUSIE

Now we can purchase some nice meat to go along with the vegetables and rice we are presently serving.

PING

I have to leave now... Lunch with Detective Grasso ... Then back to the old grind.

HOUSIE

You could eat here.

PING

I could ... But I'm not going to let Detective Grasso off the hook so easily.

HOUSIE
(to Johnny)
If you go to a Chinese restaurant, stay away from the pork fried rice.

JOHNNY
(looks like he's about to get sick)
The pork in the fried rice isn't really cat ... Is it?

HOUSIE

Millions of stray cats in New York City ... Cheaper than pork.

PING
(to Johnny)
Don't listen to Housie. I'm Chinese ... from Chinatown ...

The restaurants I frequent, take my word for it, they don't serve cat.

                    JOHNNY
But some restaurants do?

                    PING
No. That's a figment of Housie's imagination.

Johnny and Ping turn to leave.

                    HOUSIE
            (laughing)
Meow!!

                    PING
            (to Johnny)
Quick. Before he corrupts you.

Ping grabs Johnny's arm and pulls him out of the office.

EXT. CHINESE RESTAURANT - DAY

In the fogged restaurant window, fried ducks and chickens hang by their necks.

INT. CHINESE RESTAURANT - DAY

The joint is a narrow, dingy dive. The wall menu is written in Chinese and so are the table menus. All the patrons in the place are Chinese.

The kitchen is in the back; behind a swinging door.

In the background, we hear soft Chinese chatter.

Ping and Johnny sit at the last table near the kitchen.

Ping eats with chopsticks; Johnny uses a fork.

> JOHNNY
> *(looks back at the kitchen)*
> These are real Bob Uecker seats ... Best in the house.

> PING
> Who's Bob Uecker?

> JOHNNY
> *(wipes his mouth with a napkin)*
> Never mind ... He's just an old baseball player who always sits in the worst seats in the ballpark.
> *(beat)*
> Tell me something. At the soup kitchen we just left, all the people eating there were women. Why is that?

> PING
> Those women work 12 to 16 hours a day at one of the many sweatshops in Chinatown ... for much less than

minimum wage. They cannot afford to eat properly on what they earn. So we take care of them.

                    JOHNNY
So where's the men?

                    PING
The men work in restaurants all day, doing menial tasks for pennies an hour. But they eat for free ... Mostly cheap meatless rice dishes ... We get a few men early in the morning at the soup kitchen before they go to work ... It's their best meal of the day.

                    JOHNNY
We're talking about illegals here? ... Right?

                    PING
          (smirks)
You're a regular Carnac the Magnificent.

                    JOHNNY
Come on. Are things so bad in China that these poor people would leave their homeland to work like slaves in America?

                    PING
As bad as these illegal immigrants have it in America, it's a thousand times better than what they have back in China.

                    JOHNNY
Okay ... Say I buy that for a minute.
          (eats)
This fellow Housie ... What's the deal with him?

                    PING
Housie is a revered businessman in Chinatown. He runs an import/export business. Housie puts most of his profits back into the community. He funds the soup kitchen

almost entirely by himself.

                    JOHNNY
And the envelope you gave him?

                    PING
My humble contribution to the cause ... Other Chinese
business people contribute too ... When they can.
          (eats)
We take care of our own.

                    JOHNNY
You mean unlike the Italians.

                    PING
          (shrugs)
If the shoe fits.
          (puts her chopsticks on the table)
You're not working for immigration, are you?

                    JOHNNY
No. I have much more important things to do. Like
catching the real bad guys.

                    PING
          (picks up her chopsticks)
Good, I'd hate to think ...

Three TEENAGE CHINESE GANG MEMBERS rush through
the front door of the restaurant; SHOOTING AUTOMATIC
WEAPONS.

They spray the floor and ceiling with GUNFIRE.

PATRONS SCREAM.

Some are HIT BY GUNFIRE; while others dive to the floor.

A CHINESE COUPLE runs past the gunmen and out the front

door.

Johnny pulls Ping to the ground. Ping's EYEGLASSES fly off her face.

Two waiters run back toward the kitchen. One waiter is SHOT IN THE BACK and falls at Johnny's feet.

Johnny's cheek is nicked by a bullet, and a small drop of blood runs down the side of his face.

Johnny overturns his table; using it as a shield. He pulls out his gun.

JOHNNY RETURNS FIRE; KILLING TWO GUNMEN.

JOHNNY SHOOTS THE THIRD GUNMAN IN THE FOOT.

The third gunman SCREAMS in pain.

The third gunman does an about-face and quickly limps out the front door.

                    JOHNNY
                  (to Ping)
          Stay right here! Don't move!

                    PING
              (pulls out her cell phone)
          I'll call 911.

Johnny jumps to his feet. He pushes past terrified patrons and dashes out the front door.

EXT. CHINESE RESTAURANT - CONTINUOUS

Johnny rushes out of the restaurant; gun drawn.

He scans in both directions through the thick lunchtime crowd.

Johnny spots the third gunman LIMPING into a car.

The car speeds away.

Pissed off, Johnny holsters his gun and sprints back into the restaurant.

INT. CHINESE RESTAURANT - CONTINUOUS

Johnny rushes back to Ping.

> JOHNNY
> Are you okay?

> PING
> *(holding her broken eyeglasses)*
> I'm fine ... Just a little ticked off.

> JOHNNY
> Do you know why anyone would want to kill you?

> PING
> Kill me? ... Are you nuts? ...They were shooting at you!

> JOHNNY
> That's crazy! Why would Chinese gangsters want to kill a New York city cop? ... That makes no sense.

> PING
> *(wipes the blood from Johnny's cheek with a napkin)*
> It made sense to somebody.

> JOHNNY
> *(shaking his head)*
> I don't get it ... This is crazy.

> PING
> Crazy's not the word.

COPS AND PARAMEDICS rush through the front door.

                    JOHNNY
          We should have went to Forlinis' for lunch instead.

               PING
          (*stares at her broken eyeglasses*)
          From your mouth to God's ears.

INT. GRASSO RESIDENCE/DINING ROOM - NIGHT

Pete, Rita, Paulie, and Lisa are eating at the dining room table.

Johnny enters the room. A bandage is taped to his cheek.

Johnny removes his holstered gun and puts it on the credenza.

> **RITA**
> *(to Johnny)*
> What happened with your cheek?

> **JOHNNY**
> A little scratch ... I was eating lunch in a Chinese dive in
> Chinatown and some punks came in shooting.

> **PETE**
> I told you. That's why we moved to Brooklyn in the first
> place. The Chinks are shooting up the streets like
> cowboys!

> **LISA**
> I saw something about that on the Five O'clock news.
> Were you the cop who killed the two Chinese gangsters?

> **JOHNNY**
> Just call me Johnny Deadeye.

> **PAULIE**
> I saw that on TV too. One got away, didn't he?

> **JOHNNY**
> Yeah, but he's not getting around too good. I shot him in
> the foot.

> **RITA**
> Oh my God! My son gets shot eating lunch! ... What's

this world coming to?

                    JOHNNY
I'm not sure it was an accident. I was eating with Ping.
She thinks I was the intended target.

                    PAULIE
Why you?

                    JOHNNY
I don't know. Maybe you could tell me.

                    PAULIE
Me? ... I don't know nothing.

                    JOHNNY
                    (to Paulie)
Did you hear about the early morning shooting on Canal
Street? Three Chinese gangbangers got blasted. And
according to an eyewitness, the three shooters were white.

                    PAULIE
I don't know nothin' about it.

                    JOHNNY
                    (eats)
Whatever.

                    PETE
(holds his stomach; to Rita)
    Honey, could you get me some Brioschi. All this talk of
shooting is giving me agita.

INT. CHINATOWN COFFEE SHOP - NIGHT

Ah Kay, Xin Lin, and Duk Tang sit at a table; sipping cognac.

> **DUK**
> So what's this I hear about an Italian social club going up in flames?

> **AH KAY**
> Like the Towering Inferno.

> **XIN LIN**
> The Greasers were hit so hard, olive oil was flowing in the streets.

> **DUK**
> Word is, one of the Italians outside saw the person who threw the bomb.

> **AH KAY**
> So what? ... We outnumber the Italians 10-1 in Chinatown. If it comes to an all-out war, we'll kick their Guinea asses all the way back to the boot of Italy.

> **DUK**
> *(smacks Ah Kay's face)*
> And who gave the order to shoot the cop in broad daylight in Chinatown? That was damn stupid! It was all over television!

> **AH KAY**
> That cop's brother killed two of my best men. That was my way of sending a message.

> **DUK**
> Killing a cop sends a message alright. It shows how stupid you are.

AH KAY
(his head down)
Maybe I should have confirmed it with you first.

DUK
Damn right you should have. Customers were shot. One waiter's dead. Where did you get these shooters from? ... The School for the Blind?

AH KAY
It was an initiation into our gang.
(sips cognac)
They failed the test. Two are dead already and the other one is injured.

XIN LIN
I'll make sure the injured boy is taken care of too ... We have to tie up any loose ends.

DUK
(sips cognac)
Right now, it looks like a coincidence the cop was in the Chinese restaurant during the shooting. If the New York City police department finds out the truth, it puts all our businesses in jeopardy.

XIN LIN
We'll ask our contact in the Fifth Precinct what the word is about the shooting.

DUK
Still, the damage is done as far as our neighborhood being safe for tourists. And that's got to hurt the Italian businesses too ... More than ours.

AH KAY
Fuck the Italians. I say we take those greasers out ... Chinatown is our neighborhood   now.

                          DUK
          Don't be too quick. Don Vito is not stupid. But I'm damn
sure he's angry.
                    (beat)
                    And I'm angry too.
                    (curses in Chinese)

Duk THROWS the cognac glass against the wall. GLASS
SHATTERS in all directions.

EXT. CENTRAL PARK/SOFTBALL FIELD – LATE
MORNING

Bright sunshine beats down from a cloudless sky and a brisk
wind kicks up the infield sand.

Men and women are playing softball in a mixed league. A young
lady rounds third base. She slides into home plate. She's safe!

The male catcher picks her up, while her teammates CHEER.

THREE MEN sit alone in the raised metal stands.

One man is Carlo, and the other is his boss VITO PAISANO.
Vito is smoking a huge cigar.

Vito's bodyguard Philly Guns sits two rows behind them. His left
arm is in a sling and a bandage is taped to his forehead.

> VITO
> *(to Carlo)*
> So, where were you when the lights went out?

> CARLO
> We had a blackout?

> VITO
> No, moron. When our social club got bombed; where
were you?

> CARLO
> I was in the back room with your nephew Paulie.

> VITO
> And then?

> CARLO

I was knocked out cold. The next thing I knew, Paulie was dragging me out the back door.

                    VITO
You say you want a bump up to captain ... But being a captain has certain responsibilities.
          (puffs his cigar)
You should have gone back in and tried to save people ... Get them outta there.

                    CARLO
Like I said, I was knocked out cold. I wasn't thinking straight at the time.

                    VITO
Good thing Sammy the Hook was strolling by. He called 911 from his cell. Then he went inside and started pulling people out ... Like the firemen did at 9/11.
(points his thumb back at Philly Guns)
Sammy the Hook saved my man Philly Guns and a half a dozen other men.

                    CARLO
Well you know, if I had all my senses, I would have done the same thing Sammy the Hook did.

                    VITO
Maybe ... Now, let's backtrack a little.
          (puffs his cigar)
Sammy the Hook saw the people who threw the bomb ... He said they were two Chinese   gang members ... Those two mean fuckers always out in the streets terrorizing people.
          (beat)
What's their names?

                    CARLO
Chinamen bastards.

                    VITO

No. I want their names!

CARLO
I think I know who you mean.
(beat)
Ah-something is one of them ... I can't remember the name of the other one.

VITO
Do you know of any possible reason why Chinese gang members would want to torch our club?

CARLO
Not off the top of my head.

VITO
(puffs his cigar)
Not off the top of his head, he says

CARLO
Don Vito, you gotta understand. These Chinks are animals. They enjoy doing things like that.

VITO
(angry)
Don't call them Chinks! That's not nice! They're Chinese people!

CARLO
Sorry. But Chinese gang members just kill for the fun of it. They don't need a reason.

VITO
(shakes his head)
They don't need a reason, he says.

CARLO
Not like us Italians. We only do things like that when it is absolutely necessary.

VITO
(stand; hovers over Carlo)
Then tell me why it was absolutely fuckin' necessary for
my nephew Paulie and two of his fuckin' friends to whack
three Chinese gang members on Canal Street the other
fucking' night.

CARLO
Paulie? ... Nah, Paulie wouldn't do a thing like that.

VITO
(sits back down)
He wouldn't?
(beat)
And as retaliation, the Chinese then come after Paulie's
brother ... my other nephew Johnny ...who just happens
to be a fuckin' New York City police detective.

CARLO
Nah. The way I heard it, those Chinks were after some
Chinese broad who was having lunch with your nephew
the cop.

VITO
Hey, what did I just tell you? ... They're Chinese people!

CARLO
Sorry. Chinese. Not Chinks.

VITO
(points his cigar at Carlo)
Don't do it again.

CARLO
(head down)
I got it.

VITO

Look, I don't need all this aggravation. All I'm trying to do is find out what the fuck is going on in my own fuckin' neighborhood. And I don't want any trouble with the Chinese people ... We're all in this together.

                    CARLO
I'll look into it ... Find out what's going on.

                    VITO
Do just that.
            (waves his hand in disgust)
Now get the fuck out of here.

Carlo stands, and without saying another word, he totters down the steps of the metal stands.

Philly Guns hops down the steps and sits next to Vito.

                PHILLY GUNS
    Lyin' cocksucker. He left me there to die. I should rip his heart out and feed it to the dogs.

                    VITO
    Hey! I should smack you in the face for talking about another made guy like that.

                PHILLY GUNS
Sorry ... I was just talking to myself.

                    VITO
I wish I was talking to myself. I'd have a better conversation with myself than I would with any of you mooks.

                PHILLY GUNS
What's a mook?

                    VITO
Never mind.

Vito stands and Philly Guns follows suit.

                    VITO
          Let's go. If we shake a leg we can make the 12:20 Mass at
Most Precious Blood Church.

Both men quickly hop down the raised metal stands.

INT. CHINESE BAR - NIGHT

The bar is packed with CHINESE GANGSTERS and their
CHINESE GIRLFRIENDS.

The gangsters wear black leather jackets and tight jeans. The
girlfriends wear tight skirts and low-cut blouses.

All the girlfriends have spiky hairdos. Some have red hair, some
have pink hair, and others have green hair; a regular
kaleidoscope of feminine tresses.

On the stage in the back of the bar, a drunken Chinese man belts
out American karaoke with a Chinese accent.

Loud talk and laughter REVERBERATE throughout the bar.

Ah Kay sits at a table in the back near the stage. He's snorting
coke like it's legal, along with his Chinese moll, LOIS, who's
wearing a tight black skirt.

Lois' hair is spiky pink. A gun is stuffed into her skirt by her
hip, barely hidden by her open red leather jacket.

Norman enters the bar and scans the interior. He spots Ah Kay's
table.

Norman approaches Ah Kay's table. He stops and hovers over
Ah Kay, as Ah Kay snorts coke through a straw.

                    AH KAY
              (looks up, sees Norman)
        Hawaii Five-O is in the house.
              (offers Norman the straw)
        Care to indulge?
        (Ah Kay points towards his girlfriend)
        Meet Lois.

NORMAN
(ignores straw)
No thanks. I'm working.
(to Lois)
You wanna zip up that jacket? The whole world sees
you've got a gun.

LOIS
(pulls out a joint, sticks it between her pouting lips)
Fuck off.

AH KAY
(to Norman)
That's actually my gun ... My little lady always holds it
for me ... Just in case.

NORMAN
I already knew that ... And this bitch is far from little,
and not even close to being a lady.

LOIS
(to Norman)
Stop taking those big dicks up your ass. It's fuckin' up
your mouth.

NORMAN
(leans both hands on table; to Ah Kay)
Let's get to it. You're wasting my time.

AH KAY
(hands Norman an envelope)
You know what you have to do. We want it done tonight.

NORMAN
(stuffs the envelope into his inside jacket pocket)
And stop snorting that garbage ... It's making you stupid.

Ah Kay looks insulted and Lois just snarls, as Norman makes

an about face and exits the bar.

INT. UNMARKED POLICE CAR - LATE NIGHT

Norman drives. Johnny sits next to him.

> NORMAN
> *(hands Johnny an envelope)*
> That's your monthly cut from the Dukman.

> JOHNNY
> *(puts the envelope into his inside jacket pocket)*
> Thanks .... I could use the cash.

> NORMAN
> But we do have one little favor to do.

> JOHNNY
> I've got a feeling I'm not going to like this.

> NORMAN
> Relax. Everything's going to be fine.

> JOHNNY
> I hate it when people tell me to relax.

> NORMAN
> So relax, will ya?

> JOHNNY
> Moron.

EXT. CHINATOWN - NIGHT

Norman parks the unmarked car on a Chinatown street corner.

INT. UNMARKED POLICE CAR - NIGHT

> JOHNNY

(continuing)
What's going on?

NORMAN
We have to wait.

Norman takes an IPOD out of his pocket. He clips it to his belt and inserts earplugs into his ears.

JOHNNY
What the heck are you doing?

NORMAN
Listening to Louie Prima.
(sings)
C' 'NA LUNA MEZZ'U MARE MAMMA MIA M'A MARITARE.

JOHNNY
(disgusted)
Retard.

EXT. CHINATOWN - NIGHT

A LONE CHINESE GANGSTER exits a Chinese restaurant. He limps down the deserted street.

INT. UNMARKED POLICE CAR - LATE NIGHT

AS BEFORE:

The two detectives sit and wait.

Norman is still listening to iPod music.

They both spot the limping gangster.

> JOHNNY
> Hey! That's the guy I shot in the foot!

> NORMAN
> *(removes the ear plugs)*
> Let's see where he goes.
> *(puts the iPod into his pocket)*

EXT. CHINATOWN - CONTINUOUS

The UNMARKED CAR slowly follows the Chinese gangster.

The Chinese gangster turns the corner.

INT. UNMARKED POLICE CAR - CONTINUOUS

Norman stops the car and puts it in park.

> NORMAN
> *(continuing; to Johnny)*
> Let's go!

EXT. CHINATOWN - CONTINUOUS

Norman bolts out of the car. He sprints around the corner after the Chinese gangster.

Johnny exits the unmarked car and runs after Norman.

EXT. CHINATOWN - CONTINUOUS

Norman grabs the Chinese gangster by the collar.

> **CHINESE GANGSTER**
> Hey. What the fuck?

> **NORMAN**
> Shut the fuck up?

Norman pushes the Chinese gangster into a tenement building.

Johnny looks both ways. Nobody is in sight.

Johnny follows Norman into the tenement.

INT. CHINATOWN TENEMENT - CONTINUOUS

Norman pushes the Chinese gangster past the stairs and into a small alcove behind the stairs.

> **NORMAN**
> *(to the Chinese Gangster)*
> Stupid fuck.

Norman PUMMELS the Chinese gangster; using both hands.

The Chinese gangster topples to the floor and lays in a fetal position; blood dripping from his mouth.

Norman PUNCHES, then KICKS the Chinese gangster repeatedly; like a madman.

NORMAN
You fucked up big-time pal.

CHINESE GANGSTER
(spits in Norman's face)
Fuck you!

Norman pulls out his gun and PISTOL WHIPS the Chinese gangster.

Johnny rushes into the tenement and pulls Norman off the Chinese gangster.

JOHNNY
Stop ... Before you kill the guy.

NORMAN
(stands)
Okay. Check outside. Make sure the coast is clear.

JOHNNY
Alright. Now be cool.

Johnny turns and hurries towards the front door.

Johnny hears TWO GUNSHOTS. He turns around.

Norman rushes into Johnny. Then he slips his gun back in its holster.

NORMAN
Let's move!

JOHNNY
What the hell did you just do?

NORMAN
The bastard spit in my face!

JOHNNY
(grabs Norman by the collar)
So you fuckin' shoot him, you stupid bastard?

Norman yanks Johnny's hands off his collar.

NORMAN
It's too late now ... He's dead ... Let's get the hell out of here!

The two detectives dash out the tenement front door.

EXT. CHINATOWN - CONTINUOUS

Johnny and Norman rush outside.

They jump into their unmarked car; Norman gets behind the wheel.

Norman steps on the gas, hard.

The car SCREECHES away from the curb.

INT. UNMARKED POLICE CAR - CONTINUOUS

JOHNNY
You maniac bastard! ... What the hell's wrong with you?

NORMAN
How about a little ride on the Staten Island Ferry?

JOHNNY
You're crazy! You stupid Chinaman bastard!
(Lowers voice; angry)
You just killed a guy.

NORMAN
(looks at his wristwatch)

If we hurry, we can make the 4:30 ferry.

                    JOHNNY
What's with the freakin' ferry? We've got big-time
problems on our hands.

                    NORMAN
I just love those ferry franks. They're better than
Nathan's.

                    JOHNNY
               (shakes his head)
You're an idiot.

EXT. ENTRANCE TO STATEN ISLAND FERRY - LATE NIGHT

Norman parks the unmarked car next to a fire hydrant. Norman and Johnny exit the car.

> NORMAN
> Quick. Let's split. It's almost 4:30.

> JOHNNY
> You parked by a hydrant.

> NORMAN
> So what? ... I'm a cop.

They dash into the STATEN ISLAND FERRY TERMINAL.

EXT. STATEN ISLAND FERRY - LATE NIGHT

A glimmer of light peeks through the sky.

The STATEN ISLAND FERRRY glides past the STATUE OF LIBERTY.

Johnny and Norman stand on the bottom level of the ferry; outside section; back of the ferry.

Norman has earplugs in his ears and an iPod clipped to his belt. He munches on a hot dog and washes it down with a gulp of soda from a huge Styrofoam container.

> NORMAN
> *(takes earplugs out of his ears)*
> Great franks. How come you're not eating?

> JOHNNY
> I lost my appetite.

NORMAN

Hey ... Remember when they used to allow cars on the ferry?

JOHNNY

Yeah.

NORMAN

They banned cars after some jerk drove his car off the ferry into the water ... Remember?

JOHNNY

I remember.

NORMAN

Fuckin' guy was a ferry employee too ... What a dickhead.

Norman finishes his soda. He turns facing the water, then he glances towards the inside of the ferry. No one is in sight.

Norman takes the MURDER GUN out of his pocket. He snaps the lid off the Styrofoam container; puts the gun into the container and puts the lid back on the container.

Norman leans over the rail and drops the container into the water.

The container bobs; then disappears into the deep.

JOHNNY
(leans over rail)
What the fuck? ...

NORMAN

That gun was a throwaway ... Untraceable ... But I'm not taking any chances.

JOHNNY

Why in God's name did you kill that guy? He wasn't resisting arrest.

NORMAN

I didn't plan on making an arrest. Those weren't my orders.

JOHNNY

From who?

NORMAN

What difference does it make? There's one less punk killer on the streets of Chinatown. That's not a bad thing.

JOHNNY

He was one of the shooters in the restaurant. We could have put him in jail for a very long time.

NORMAN

That would have been a waste of taxpayer money ... And that's not what we were getting paid for anyway.

JOHNNY

That's bullshit! ... I was getting paid to look the other way while the Chinese gangs ran a little gambling ... The Italians pay us too ... to do the same thing with them ... I was not paid to be an accessory to murder.

NORMAN

You take money from those Chinese gangs, you do what they tell you to do. Period.

JOHNNY
(gets in Norman's face)
No more fuckin' surprises! You hear me! You stepped way out of bounds on this one!

NORMAN

What are you worried about? We just got away with murder.

JOHNNY

We did what? ... Do you have a roach in your pocket, or something ... I had nothing to do with this.

NORMAN
(pulls out a joint)
Yeah. I have a roach. Got a match?

JOHNNY

Don't be a jerkoff.
(leans on the rail facing the water)
The way things have washed, whether I like it or not, I'm an accomplice to fuckin' murder. And you, you fuck, were responsible for getting me into this mess.

NORMAN
(puts joint back into his pocket)
Don't worry. Nobody's going to miss that prick.

JOHNNY
(holds his head in his hands)
I just wish this night was over.

NORMAN

I need another frank. Want one?

JOHNNY

I hope that gun doesn't wash up somewhere.

NORMAN

Wash up where? The ocean swallowed up the evidence. There must be a million guns in the water here.

JOHNNY

Yeah. You're right. I'm just freaked out.
(beat)

Fuckin' murderers. That's what we are. You pulled the trigger, but I'm just as guilty as you are … For not arresting you on the spot.

NORMAN
Whatever… Hot dog time. Best dogs in town. Better than Katz Deli.

Norman turns and heads inside the ferry to get more hotdogs.

INT. CHINATOWN CHURCH - EARLY MORNING

A PRIEST, aided by TWO ALTAR BOYS, performs MASS at the altar.

The first two rows are filled with OLD CHINESE WOMEN and OLD ITALIAN WOMEN dressed in black, wearing black kerchiefs over their heads. A handful of other parishioners dot the pews.

The priest's LATIN CHANTING reverberates throughout the church.

Johnny kneels in the last pew in the back of the church; praying.

While Mass is still in service, Johnny makes the sign of the cross. He stands and heads for the back door of the church.

Johnny stops at the poor box. He removes the envelope Norman had given him the night before and drops it into the poor box.

Johnny dips his hand in the holy water and makes the sign of the cross, as he genuflects.

Johnny exits the church.

INT. CHINESE SOUP KITCHEN - DAY

Ping, wearing a white apron, stands behind the counter serving food to a queue of CHINESE WOMEN.

Norman enters the soup kitchen. He grabs a tray and stands in line.

When Norman reaches to where Ping is standing, he sneaks Ping an envelope.

FLASHBACK TO:

INT. CHINATOWN TENEMENT APARTMENT - NIGHT

AS IN SCENE # 1:

The Chinese girl is chained to the radiator.

The Chinese gangster hovers over her.

> CHINESE GANGSTER
> The rent is now due.
> *(beat)*
> Ready to pay?

WE NOW REALIZE THE CHINESE GIRL WAS PING.

BACK TO THE PRESENT:

Ping slips the envelope into her apron pocket.

Ping spoons food into a dish and places the dish on Norman's tray.

Norman nods to Ping. He continues walking with his tray of food past the counter and takes a seat at an empty table.

EXT. JIMMY'S CORNER BAR - NIGHT

An INTOXICATED MAN AND WOMAN exit the bar, which is located fifty feet east of TIMES SQUARE.

We see the Times Square lights in the background and hear the LOUD NOISE of speeding traffic.

INT. JIMMY'S CORNER - NIGHT

There's a long, narrow bar with several tables in the back. The lights are dim and the walls are filled with boxing photos.

The jukebox BLARES Motown.

HOOKERS, PIMPS, and TOURISTS mingle at the bar. Everybody is having a grand old time.

The BARTENDER is a large black man, with droopy eyes and a scowl on his face. He's arguing with a WELL-DRESSED DRUNK sitting at the bar.

                    BARTENDER
          I'm telling you ... Muhammad Ali was the greatest.

                    DRUNKEN BAR CUSTOMER
                    (holding his drink on the bar)
          Rocky Marciano would have kicked Ali's black butt back
to Africa.

                    BARTENDER
          Ali was born in Louisville, Kentucky.

                    DRUNKEN BAR CUSTOMER
          Same fucking thing.

                    BARTENDER

(takes drink away from drunken customer)
That's it for you ... You've had enough.

DRUNKEN BAR CUSTOMER
Hey man, that ain't right.

CUT TO:

Johnny and Paulie sit at a small table in the back.

JOHNNY
(sips drink)
Well little brother, you really screwed up big this time.
Because of what you did on Canal Street, I now have the
Chinese Gangs up my ass.
(beat)
How could you do this to me?

PAULIE
I'm sorry. I got in deep gambling ... I thought this was my
way out.

JOHNNY
What are you talking about?

PAULIE
With my cut from the Snakehead's smuggling operation, I
could have paid all my debts. I would have been free and
clear.

JOHNNY
You asked the Chinese gangs for a cut of their
Snakehead's business?

PAULIE
I didn't. Carlo did ... But it was basically my idea .... And
the Chinks basically told us to go fuck ourselves ... I was
there at the sit-down.

JOHNNY
Who else was there?

PAULIE
Me and Carlo. And Duk Tang and his flunkey, Ah Kay.

JOHNNY
And Uncle Vito said this was okay?

PAULIE
I didn't talk to Uncle Vito. He's the top guy ... You don't do things that way in the mob. You use the chain of command ... I went to my boss Carlo.

JOHNNY
Chain of command, my ass.

PAULIE
Look, Carlo's my boss. In this life, you do whatever your boss tells you to do ... No questions asked ... And you don't go over his head ... Ever.

JOHNNY
Look, this is bullshit. Uncle Vito is family. He's our blood ... our uncle ... Of course we can talk to him directly without going through that greedy fuck Carlo.

PAULIE
I don't know ... That doesn't sound right to me.

JOHNNY
(massages both of his temples)
Well, I know what I gotta do now.

PAULIE
What? ... What are you gonna do?

JOHNNY
(head down)

Drink your drink ... I'm still thinking.

INT. FLEABAG HOTEL ROOM IN MANHATTAN – NIGHT

Norman gets dressed while a CHINESE PROSTITUTE sits on the bed.

The Chinese prostitute wears only her bra and panties, and she's counting the money Norman has just given her.

> ### CHINESE PROSTITUTE
> Hey mister! You're a hundred dollars short! We agreed on two hundred, not one hundred. dollars!

> ### NORMAN
> (*angry*)
> You're lucky you're getting paid at all.

Norman takes out his wallet and flashes his police shield.

> ### NORMAN
> (*continuing*)
> You're lucky I don't pull you in.

> ### CHINESE PROSTITUTE
> Typical cop. You guys always want something for nothing … Even pussy.

The black prostitute puts the money into her bra. She jumps off the bed and starts dressing; with her back to Norman.

From his pants pocket, Norman pulls out a small GUN with a SILENCER attached to it.

HE SHOOTS THE CHINESE PROSTITUTE IN THE BACK OF THE HEAD.

The gunshot is so muffled, it sounds like someone just popped a small balloon.

The Chinese prostitute falls flat on her face.

Norman paces to where the Chinese prostitute is lying. He turns her body over. Her dead eyes are wide open and bloods spills from the back of her head, forming a large puddle on the hotel room floor.

Norman reaches into the Chinese prostitute's bra, removes the hundred dollars, and puts the money into his pants pocket.

> NORMAN
> Like I said before … That's one less whore the city has to worry about.

Norman slips the gun back into his pants pocket. He puts on his sports jacket and exits the hotel room.

INT. CHINESE SOUP KITCHEN/OFFICE - DAY

Housie is sitting at his desk.

Ping enters and hands Housie a white envelope. Housie opens the envelope and counts the money.

> HOUSIE
> It's a little short ... Maybe Norman is holding out.

> PING
> That doesn't surprise me ... But there's one sure way to find out.

> HOUSIE
> Be careful. Those Circle of Boys are very bad people.
> *(beat)*
> They kill just for the fun of it.

Ping opens her purse and pulls out a gun.

> PING
> *(shows gun to Housie)*
> I've been through too much in my life to let them stop me now.

> HOUSIE
> Just be careful.

> PING
> I will ... Don't worry ... I've got everything covered.

Ping exits Housie's office.

INT. CHINATOWN APARTMENT - DAY

Johnny enters the apartment and is greeted by TWO FBI
AGENTS, both wearing FBI identification tags on chains around
their necks.

> ### FBI AGENT NO. 1
> (*to Johnny*)
> Give me the envelope Norman gave to you ... I need it as

evidence.

> ### JOHNNY
> The envelope is gone.

> ### FBI AGENT NO. 2
> What do you mean it's gone?

> ### JOHNNY
> I put it in a poor box at Transfiguration Church.

> ### FBI AGENT NO. 1
> (*to FBI agent No. 2*)
> I wondered what he was doing in that church.

> ### FBI AGENT NO 2.
> (*to Johnny*)
> You expect us to believe a bullshit story like that?

> ### JOHNNY
> I don't give a fuck what you believe ... The poor people
> need that money more than the government ... I call it my
> redistribution of wealth ... Ask your boss Obama what
> that means.

> ### FBI AGENT NO. 2
> This has to go into my report ... It won't look good for

you.

JOHNNY

Who gives a fuck? ... Now let's get going. I don't have all day.

Johnny takes off his ROLEX WRISTWATCH and hands it to FBI agent No. 1

FBI agent No. 1 takes off the back of the Rolex. Using tweezers, he pulls out a tiny transmitter.

FBI AGENT NO. 1
(hands transmitter and watch to FBI Agent No. 2)
That transmitter is fried. No wonder we weren't getting anything.

Using tweezers, FBI agent No. 2 puts a new transmitter into the Rolex. Then he snaps shut the back of the watch.

FBI AGENT NO. 2
(gives the watch back to Johnny)
Now it's good to go ... Don't fuck this up.

JOHNNY
(puts the Rolex back on his wrist)
Wonderful ... You guys are geniuses ... You're not as stupid as everyone thinks you are.

FBI AGENT NO. 2.
(ignores Johnny's remark)
Duk Tang is going to request a meeting with you and Norman soon. We already have enough on your partner to put him away for a long time ... But we want Duk Tang.

FBI AGENT NO. 1
So be careful and don't fuck this up.

JOHNNY

You said that already.
>   *(beat)*
>   Look. Let's get one thing straight ... I hate the fucking

FBI.
>   *(beat)*
>   You know what FBI stands for?

FBI AGENT NO. 2.
>   Federal Bureau of Investigation.

JOHNNY
>   No ... Famous ... But ... Incompetent.

FBI AGENT NO. 1
>   Very funny.

JOHNNY
>   All you guys think you're J. Edgar Hoover ... And he was

an incompetent prick too.

FBI AGENT NO. 1
>   (to Johnny)
>   You're an asshole.

JOHNNY
>   Look, I only agreed to work with you jerks because my
>   boss in A. I. D. is a stand-up guy. It was against my better
>   judgment ... But he talked me into it.
>   *(beat)*
>   But the minute this investigation is over, I'm through
>   with you pieces of shit ... You got it?

Johnny turns around. He opens the apartment door, exits the
room, and SLAMS THE DOOR behind him.

INT. GRASSO RESIDENCE/DINING ROOM - NIGHT

Johnny, Paulie, and Pete sit at the dining room table. Two bottles of red wine stand on the table in front of them.

> PETE
> *(extends glass to Paulie)*
> Pour me a glass, will ya ... I need to get drunk.

> PAULIE
> *(pours wine, hands glass to Pete)*
> Just one glass. According to mom, your blood pressure is going through the roof.

> PETE
> Keep tabs on me ... And you're going through the roof.

> JOHNNY
> What do you say, guys? ... Pistols at fifty paces?

The front doorbell RINGS. Pete gets up from the table. He walks to the front door and opens it.

Vito enters.

> PETE
> *(hugs Vito)*
> My brother-in-law Vito graces our humble abode.
> *(takes Vito's arm)*
> Come in and sit.

Johnny and Paulie take turns hugging Uncle Vito. Then...

Vito sits at the head of the dining room table.

> VITO
> Where's the food? I'm starving.

Rita and Lisa enter the dining room. Both women are wearing cooking aprons.

Vito stands and greets the two women.

> ### RITA
> *(kisses Vito's cheek)*
> My handsome brother.

> ### VITO
> *(hugs Rita)*
> You're as beautiful as ever.

> ### PAULIE
> *(whispers to Johnny)*
> Get me a paddle ... It's getting deep in here.

> ### LISA
> *(hugs Uncle Vito and kisses his cheek)*
> Uncle Vito. It's wonderful to see you.

> ### VITO
> *(to Lisa)*
> Gorgeous, just like your mother.

> ### PAULIE
> *(under his breath)*
> More bullshit.

> ### RITA
> *(to Paulie)*
> Hey! Watch your mouth ... No cursing at the dining room table. Remember?
> *(to Vito)*
> We have to get back into the kitchen ... Lisa is helping me with the manicot.

Rita and Lisa return to the kitchen.

VITO
(to Pete)
It's about time you invited me to dinner ... It's nice to be with my family ... You should invite me here more often.

PETE
Vito ... we know how busy you are in Manhattan. We hate to bother you.

VITO
Bother me? ... Nonsense ... You're all the family I've got.

JOHNNY
(to Vito)
A little wine, Uncle Vito?

VITO
Sure. Is that a Chianti?

JOHNNY
Bolla Bardolino ... The best.

Johnny pours Uncle Vito a glass of Bolla.

PAULIE
I prefer Corvo myself.

PETE
(sharply: to Paulie)
Then buy some Corvo! ... You've gotta spring for some cash once in a while. You're as tight as a clam's ass.

VITO
I think Paulie has been springing a little bit too much lately ... The springs are coming out of his brains.

PETE
I got a feeling I don't want to hear this.

Vito leans across the table and Paulie leans towards him. Their faces are less than a foot apart.

                    VITO
               (whispers to Paulie)
     What the hell were you thinking?
               (beat)
     You know ... That thing there on Canal Street ... Near the
Holland Tunnel.
               (pinches Paulie's cheek)
     What are you? A cowboy or somethin'?

                    PAULIE
               (leans back)
     Uncle Vito, you've to believe me. That was not my call.

                    VITO
               (leans back)
     But it was your original idea, wasn't it?

                    PAULIE
     Yeah, it was ... I had this idea about extorting money
     from the Chinks. I ran it past Carlo, who is my boss, and
     he liked the idea. I figured he ran it past you and got your
     okay.

                    VITO
               (to Paulie)
     They're Chinese people. Don't call them Chinks.

                    PAULIE

The Chinese gangs are making tons of money smuggling Chinese
human cargo from China into the United States ... For as much
as fifty large a head.

                    VITO
     So ... What does that have to do with us?

PAULIE

I figured it's our streets they're crowding with thousands of fuckin' Chin ...

VITO

Don't say it ...

PAULIE
(hesitates)
Chinese people.

VITO

That's better.

PAULIE

So why shouldn't we get our cut?

VITO
(sips wine)
Number one ... That's for me to decide ... Number two, considering number one, why didn't you just come to me in the first place?

PAULIE

I followed the chain of command. I went to Carlo ... Those are the rules, ain't they?

VITO

Yes, normally those are the rules ... But you're my nephew. Fuck the rules!
(beat)
What happened next?

PAULIE

Carlo called for a sitdown with Duk Tang. I was there. The Dukman turned us down flat.

VITO

This is the first time I'm hearing about this.

PAULIE

What? ... Carlo never told you about any of this?

VITO

Not a word ... If he had asked me, I would have turned him down flat. That's Chinese business. It's none of our affair.

PETE
(to Vito)
Maybe Carlo didn't tell you because he wanted the money all for himself.

VITO

Could be ... You can never tell with a prick like Carlo what he's thinking.

PAULIE

I'd like to get my hands around Carlo's neck.

VITO
(to Paulie)
Calm down ... Carlo's a made guy. You can't talk about him like that ... Especially in front of me ... Those are the rules too.
(beat)
Until now.
(sips wine)
In fact, that's one of the reasons I'm here ... Besides dining with my wonderful family.

JOHNNY

I think I know where this is heading.
(gets up from his chair)
Uncle Vito ... I'm a cop ... Do you want me to leave the room?

                    VITO
No, of course not. You're my nephew.
          (smiles)
You're not going to arrest me, are you?

                    JOHNNY
No, of course not.

                    VITO
Then sit down.
          (points to Johnny's wrist)
I see you're not wearing the Rolex I gave you. What did
you do? Lose it?

                    JOHNNY
          (sits)
I only wear the Rolex when I'm on the job.

                    VITO
Smart boy.

                    PAULIE
Rolex watch? ... What's going on here?

                    VITO
Nothing. Mind your own business.

                    PETE
          (to Paulie)
Yeah. Mind your own business.

                    VITO
Before the girls come back, I want to get this out of the
way.

                    JOHNNY
          (kidding)
Someone's getting shot.

Vito reaches across the table and holds Paulie's two hands in his two hands.

                         VITO
                    (to Paulie)
You're getting into too much trouble. I need to keep an
eye on you. And the best way to do that is to give you your
button ... You'll answer directly to me ... Carlo will be out
of the picture completely.
                    (beat)
What do you say?

                         PAULIE
I don't know what to say.

                         VITO
You can say no and there will be no hard feelings ...
You're still my nephew.

                         PAULIE
I'm a little overwhelmed here ... Could I think it over?

                         VITO
Sure. Think it over ... Take your time ... But I have
something you might want to do to make some easy
dough.
                    (beat)
How much do you owe Carlo?

                         PAULIE
Fifty large.

                         VITO
A man of honor always pays his debts ... Maybe I can help
you.

                         PAULIE
How?

JOHNNY
Easy guys. There's a cop sitting here.

VITO
(to Paulie)
I'll tell you after dinner. You come with me into the city ...
We'll talk.

Rita tramps into the room carrying a large tray of antipasto.

RITA
Start with this ... Lisa and I are still working on the
manicot and meatballs.

Rita exits the room.

PETE
Great! Let's dig in!

Johnny fills everyone's glass with wine.

VITO
(raises his glass)
To famiglia!

JOHNNY, PETE AND PAULIE
(in unison)
To famiglia!

INT. PING'S TRAVEL AGENCY - DAY

Ping is sitting behind her desk, doing paperwork.

Johnny enters. He's wearing his ROLEX.

> JOHNNY
> How about I take you out to lunch? ... I still owe you one.

> PING
> I don't know. The last time you took me to lunch, I wound up spitting out my egg foo young.

> JOHNNY
> Don't worry ... I know the perfect place.

EXT. COLUMBUS PARK - CHINATOWN - DAY

Ping and Johnny sit on a park bench; eating hot Italian sandwiches.

Clusters of people, both Chinese and Caucasian, mill about. In the background, old Chinese women perform their kung foo exercises.

Cooing pidgins flock throughout the park; looking for food.

> JOHNNY
> *(holds a hot sandwich in one hand)*
> So tell me, what you know about Snakeheads?

> PING
> *(takes a bite of her sandwich)*
> Why would I know anything about Snakeheads?

> JOHNNY
> Because you do ... I'm a cop. Remember?

PING
So you know more about me than I thought.

JOHNNY
Just a little.

PING
(takes a bite of her sandwich)
Well to start with, there are Snakeheads and then there are Facilitators.

JOHNNY
Whoa! Facilitators ...What does that even mean?

PING
The Snakeheads you know all about. If they are not paid on time, they do horrible things to poor the Chinese immigrants whom they smuggle into the United States.

JOHNNY
That we know.

PING
Then there are Chinese people ... upstanding businessmen and businesswomen ... who help poor Chinese people come into America.

JOHNNY
What exactly do you mean by help?

PING
They help by bribing officials at the immigration checkpoints ... Or by using forged documents to get Chinese people into America ... Nobody gets hurt.

JOHNNY
That's still against the law.

PING
(*angry*)
Whose law? ... Not our law. Our people are just trying to survive.

JOHNNY
Ok, I'll let that one pass ... But who pays for this? ...The Facilitators?

PING
Sometimes they do ... Like when the people being smuggled in don't have the money to pay for things like the forged documents.

JOHNNY
Or bribes.

PING
Or bribes.

JOHNNY
(*takes a bite of his sandwich*)
Forgive me if I think what you're telling me is fantasy land ... Or something out of the Twilight Zone.

PING
Think what you like. But it's all true.

JOHNNY
All right ... Tell me more about these Facilitators.

PING
(*takes a bite of her sandwich*)
The Facilitators are mostly rich business people living in Chinatown. In addition to providing the planning and the routes, they give the illegal immigrants interest-free loans to cover expenses they incur to enter and stay in the United States.

JOHNNY
Interest-free loans? ... That's a new concept in America.

PING
The loans usually originate in China.

JOHNNY
(takes a bite of his sandwich)
Which was a Communist country.

PING
Which still is an oppressive country to the poor.

JOHNNY
So America is better for these people being smuggled in?
... Better than their homes in China.

PING
Much better.

JOHNNY
That's hard to believe.

PING
When the illegals get into America, the Facilitators find
them jobs; either in restaurants, or in factories.

JOHNNY
Where they work 80 hours a week for much less than
minimum wage.

PING
The system isn't perfect ... But I'm telling you, no matter
how bad the jobs are the illegals get in America, it's a
hundred times better than the life they live in China.

JOHNNY
But it must take them years to pay back these loans.

PING

Not really ... Remember, the Facilitators make no money
on this. The expenses may be five, ten thousand dollars.
Tops. The illegals pay back the money they owe as fast as
they can. And they always do ... It's a matter of honor.

JOHNNY

Look, I see where you're coming from. But these
Facilitators are still breaking the laws here in America.
You can't convince me otherwise.

PING

Who cares about the American laws? These laws are
applied arbitrarily anyway. The Facilitators feel they are
doing nothing wrong. They feel they are performing a
public service to the Chinese-American community...
And the community agrees with them.

JOHNNY

I'd have a hard time getting that past my boss in the Fifth
Precinct.

PING

People have to do what they have to do to survive ...
What's wrong with people striving for a better life?

JOHNNY

Well, for one thing, these people can enter the country
legally. We have the mechanism here in American for
them to do just that. They have to fill out the proper
forms and go through the proper channels.

PING

Oh please! Since 9/11, the immigration movement in the
United States has been at a standstill. American
immigration officials think everyone's a terrorist.

JOHNNY

Turn around.

(he turns toward the southwest)
Look at the sky. What don't you see?

PING
(she turns too)
I know ... The World Trade Center ... It's gone.

JOHNNY
That's right ... After 9/11 you think the United States wants to make it easy for foreigners to come into this country? ... We just can't take that risk.

PING
I understand your point ... And that's exactly why the Facilitators are needed. And why it's imperative to crack down on the Snakeheads who are extortionists, rapists, and murderers.

JOHNNY
(takes a bite of his sandwich)
Okay ... Let me chew on that one for a while.

EXT. TRUCK REST STOP - JERSEY TURNPIKE - LATE
NIGHT

An ISOLATED TRUCK is parked 100 yards from the
restrooms. The DRIVER is sleeping behind the wheel.

A CAR parks next to the truck. THREE HIJACKERS wearing
Halloween masks exit the car.

HIJACKER No. 1 knocks on the truck driver side window.

The driver awakes and rolls down his window.

Hijacker No. 1 puts a gun in the truck driver's face.

> HIJACKER NO. 1
> *(Screams at the truck driver)*
> Get out of the truck! ... Now! ... Hands behind your head!

The scared truck driver exits the truck; his hands interlocked
behind his head.

The hijackers tie the truck driver's hands behind his back with
rope. Then they put duct tape over his mouth to keep him quiet.

HIJACKER NO. 2 opens the driver's door of the car. He gets
behind the wheel.

Hijacker No. 1 opens the back door of the car. Pushes the truck
driver into the back seat of the car.

Hijacker No. 1 gets into the back seat next to the truck driver.

HIJACKER NO. 3 jumps into the truck. He gets behind the
wheel and takes off his mask.

We see it's JIMMY RYAN.

Jimmy puts the truck in gear and drives back onto the Jersey Turnpike.

INT. CAR - LATE NIGHT - CONTINUOUS

Hijacker No. 1 sticks a gun into the truck driver's ribs.

> ### HIJACKER NO. 1
> *(to the truck driver)*
> No funny stuff and you'll get out of this alive.

Hijacker No. 2 drives the car out of the rest area.

EXT. SECLUDED AREA – NEXT TO THE JERSEY TURNPIKE - LATE NIGHT

Hijacker No. 1 gets out of the car. He opens the back door of the car and drags the truck driver out of the back seat.

Hijacker No. 2 gets out of the car. He pats down the truck driver and finds the truck driver's wallet.

Hijacker No. 2 pulls the truck driver's driver's license out of the wallet. Hijacker No. 2 hands the driver's license to Hijacker No. 1.

Hijacker No. 1 peers at the truck driver's driver's license

> ### HIJACKER NO. 1
> *(to the truck driver)*
> Now we know where you live ... Don't be a hero.
> *(he puts the license into his pants pocket)*
> Forget all about this. Or we'll come looking for you ...
And your family.

The truck driver makes muffled sounds.

Hijacker No. 1 puts the wallet back into the truck driver's pants pocket.

Hijacker No. 2 covers the truck driver's nose and mouth with a cloth soaked in ether.

The truck driver loses consciousness and FALLS TO THE GROUND.

The hijackers drag the truck driver behind a tree. They place him in a sitting position and wrap ROPE around the truck driver and the tree. Hijacker No. 2 ties the loose ends of the rope behind the tree tightly with an intricate knot.

> HIJACKER NO. 2
> He ain't going nowhere.

> HIJACKER NO. 1
> Let's split.

Hijacker No. 1 takes off his MASK.

We see it's PAULIE.

Hijacker No. 2 takes off his MASK.

We see it's BILLY THE POLARK.

> PAULIE
> My Uncle Vito was right … This score was a cinch.

Paulie and Billy the Polark get into the car; Billy behind the wheel and Paulie in the passenger seat.

The car exits the secluded area.

INT. UNMARKED POLICE CAR - NIGHT

Norman drives. Johnny sits next to him.

> **NORMAN**
> I just got a call on my cell ... Duk Tang wants to meet us right away.

> **JOHNNY**
> What for?

> **NORMAN**
> Who knows? ... It will only take a minute.

> **JOHNNY**
> What if we get a police call?

> **NORMAN**
> Don't worry. I said this will be quick.

> **JOHNNY**
> Okay. But stop at Forlinis first ... I've got to make a head stop.

EXT. PAY PHONE - NIGHT

Carlo is talking on the pay phone.

> ### CARLO
> Paulie, I've got good news for you.
> *(beat)*
> Dress up in your best suit.

> ### PAULIE
> *(voice on phone)*
> What's this all about?

> ### CARLO
> No questions. I'll pick you up in an hour.

Carlo hangs up the phone.

INT. FORLINIS RESTAURANT - BATHROOM - NIGHT

The bathroom is empty.

INT- FORLINIS BATHROOM STALL - NIGHT

Johnny speaks softly into his Rolex wristwatch.

> **JOHNNY**
> This is John Grasso ... Detective first grade ... New York
> City Police Department ... And I'm consenting to record
> my conversation with Duk Tang, Detective Norman
> Wong, and others as-yet unknown.

Johnny exits the stall and goes to the sink.

Johnny washes his face and hands. He removes a few paper
towels from the bathroom towel dispenser and wipes his hands
dry.

> **JOHNNY**
> *(continuing; stares into the mirror.)*
> It's Showtime.

Johnny straightens his tie. He shrugs his shoulders like a
gangster in a 1930's movie and exits the bathroom.

EXT. GRASSO RESIDENCE - NIGHT

A LINCOLN TOWN CAR pulls into the driveway. Carlo gets out of the front passenger seat.

Philly Guns get out the driver's car door. His left arm is in a SLING.

Paulie walks out the front door of his house. He's wearing his best suit; with a tacky mob tie and a matching pocket handkerchief.

Carlo and Philly Guns take turns hugging Paulie and kissing him on both cheeks.

> CARLO
> *(to Paulie)*
> You look good, kid ... Today is your lucky day.

> PAULIE
> (nervous)
> I hope you're right.

Carlo opens the front passenger door. Paulie slides into the front passenger seat.

Philly Guns slips into the driver's seat of the car and Carlo slides into the back seat.

Philly Guns turns the ignition key and the car hums to life.

INT. LINCOLN – NIGHT - CONTINUOUS

> PAULIE
> *(to Philly Guns)*
> How can you drive with one hand?

                    PHILLY GUNS
            Very slowly and very carefully.
                    (beat)
            You got a problem with that?

                      PAULIE
            No ... Not at all.

                      CARLO
                (From the back seat)
            Hey, cut the chatter. We've got some serious business to
take care of.

Philly Guns glances behind him. He puts the car in reverse and
backs out of the driveway. He puts the car into drive and the car
blends into traffic.

INT. CHINESE RESTAURANT - NIGHT

Ah Kay and Xin Lin open the front door. Johnny and Norman
enter.

Ah Kay leads the detectives to a side door.

> AH KAY
> *(opens door)*
> After you.

> NORMAN
> *(peeks down the steps)*
> Looks like a fuckin' cave.

The two detectives head down the steps, followed by Ah Kay and
Xin Lin.

INT. CHINESE RESTAURANT/BASEMENT – NIGHT -
CONTINUOUS

Dim lighting. No furniture, except for a RECTANGULAR
TABLE set in the middle of the room; with two chairs facing two
other chairs.

Duk Tang sits on one side of the rectangular table. Ping sits next
to him.

Ping is wearing a black leather jacket and tight jeans; typical
Chinese gangster/girlfriend – type attire.

She is not wearing her usual black-rimmed Christian Dior
glasses.

Johnny and Norman enter the room, followed by Ah Kay and
Xin Lin.

JOHNNY
(to Ping)
What are you doing here?

PING
You'll find out soon enough.

DUK TANG
(to Johnny)
I see you know Sister Ping
(points to the two chairs opposite him)
Gentlemen, please be seated.

The two detectives sit opposite Duk Tang and Ping.

Ah Kay and Xin Lin stand menacingly behind them. Their arms folded across their chests; like big-time bodyguards.

DUK TANG
Would anyone like some tea? ... Or maybe some cognac?

JOHNNY
No ... We're good.

DUK TANG
Then let's get down to business ... Detective Grasso, may I see your wristwatch?

Johnny extends his arm exposing the ROLEX.

JOHNNY
It's a Rolex.

DUK TANG
That I can see ... Now take it off and hand it to me.

Johnny takes off the Rolex and hands it across the table to Duk Tang.

Ah Kay saunters around the table.

Duk Tang gives Ah Kay the wristwatch.

Ah Kay drops the wristwatch to the floor, and STOMPS it into LITTLE PIECES.

A TRANSMITTER is clearly visible inside the crushed Rolex.

> NORMAN
> What the hell's going on here?

> DUK TANG
> In due time, Detective ... In due time.

EXT. ITALIAN SOCIAL CLUB - NIGHT

The Lincoln Town Car parks in front of a hydrant.

Carlo, Philly Guns, and Paulie exit the car.

An ITALIAN MOBSTER guards the front door to the club. He's so tall and wide, he obscures the entrance to the social club.

Philly Guns hands the huge Italian mobster the keys to the Lincoln Town Car.

> **PHILLY GUNS**
> Take care of this for me ... Will ya?

> **ITALIAN MOBSTER**
> No problem, Philly.

Carlo enters the club; followed by Paulie and Philly Guns.

INT. CHINESE RESTAURANT/BASEMENT - NIGHT

AS BEFORE:

Duk Tang and Ping sit on one side of the rectangular table. Johnny and Norman sit opposite them.

Ah Kay and Xin Lin stand behind the detectives.

> **DUK TANG**
> *(to Norman)*
> Killing comes easy to you ... Doesn't it, Norman?

> **NORMAN**
> I do my best ... It's just a job ... Like any other job.

> **DUK**

And because of your unmatched ruthlessness, you have been a very important chess piece in my organization.

                    NORMAN
Like I said ... I do my best.

                    DUK TANG
However, it has come to my attention that you have spun out of control. And now you have cost me money and much prestige ... Face, as we Chinese like to call it.

                    NORMAN
Cost you money and prestige? ... How?

                    DUK TANG
You raped and killed a young Chinese prostitute in a hotel. This young girl was under my protection and now you have to pay for her loss.

                    NORMAN
                    (*nervous*)
You're crazy! ... I didn't kill your Chinese whore!

                    DUK TANG
Sorry, but that's simply not true.
                    (*beat*)
Since this young girl was one of mine, she was followed at all times. You were seen entering the hotel with her and you were seen leaving alone.
(*nods at Ah Kay and Xin Lin*)
Right, gentlemen.

Norman turns around. Ah Kay and Xin Lin both smile at him, wickedly.

                    NORMAN
                    (stands, fists balled)
Fuck you! Fuck you all !

Norman turns and charges Ah Kay and Xin Lin.

Ah Kay pulls out a GUN WITH A SILENCER and SHOOTS NORMAN TWICE IN THE CHEST. The gunshots sound like air flying from a pea shooter.

Norman slumps to the floor.

AH KAY SHOOTS NORMAN TWICE MORE; both times in the head.

Norman's body wiggles; then stops moving. He lays there; dead.

> DUK TANG
> *(to Johnny)*
> And now you Detective ... What do you propose I should do with you?

INT. ITALIAN SOCIAL CLUB - NIGHT

Carlo enters the social club; followed by Paulie and Philly Guns.

Vito stands, facing the three men. He has a mountainous bodyguard on each side of him.

> VITO
> *(points to a side door)*
> Welcome gentlemen ... The meeting is in the basement.

Carlo comes forward to hug Vito.

> CARLO
> Don Vito.

> VITO
> *(backs away)*
> Not this time, Carlo.

With his good hand, Philly Guns pulls out a gun. He aims over Paulie's shoulder, and ...

SHOOTS CARLO IN THE BACK.

Paulie recoils; his hands over his ears.

Carlo falls to his knees and turns towards Philly Guns.

PHILLY GUNS SHOOTS CARLO TWICE MORE IN THE CHEST.

Carlo falls onto this back.

Philly Guns leans over Carlo, and;

PUTS TWO MORE BULLETS IN CARLO'S HEAD.

PHILLY GUNS
(spits on Carlo's dead body)
Rat bastard! You left me for dead!

Paulie just stands there; petrified.

VITO
(to his two bodyguards)
Take this trash out back. There's a car waiting ... Then
come back here and clean up this mess.

Paulie whips out a handkerchief from his inside suit jacket
pocket and wipes his brow with the handkerchief.

PAULIE
Damn ... I didn't expect THIS.

VITO
(to Paulie)
You were worried? Do you think your Uncle Vito would
do you any harm?
(points to Philly Guns)
Meet your new boss.

PAULIE
(hugs Philly Guns)
Congratulations, Philly.

PHILLY GUNS
Same to you kid.

Vito's two bodyguards roll open a TARPAULIN next to Carlo's
body. They flip Carlo's body onto the tarpaulin; then fold the
tarpaulin around the Carlo's body.

The two bodyguards drag Carlo's tarpaulin-wrapped body out
the back door.

VITO
(motions to the side door)
Let's go downstairs ... We have business to take care of.
(to Philly Guns)
I have the needle ... Did you bring the religious card and
the matches.

PHILLY GUNS
(taps his breast pocket)
Right here, boss.

VITO
Which saint's card did you bring?

PHILLY GUNS
(shrugs)
I dunno ... St. Joseph, I think ... Maybe St. Peter ... The
saints all look the same to me anyway.

VITO
(shakes his head in disgust)
Let's go downstairs ... I need a fuckin' drink.

INT. CHINESE RESTAURANT/BASEMENT – NIGHT

AS BEFORE:

Norman's dead body is lying on the floor.

Johnny sits opposite Dunk Tang and Ping.

Ah Kay and Xin Lin stand behind Johnny.

> **DUK TANG**
> *(to Johnny)*
> So I ask you again ... What do you propose I should do
with you?

> **JOHNNY**
> I could use a little vacation.
> *(to Ping)*
> Hey, Sister Ping. Could you hook me up with a nice long
trip to China?

> **DUK TANG**
> You are going on a nice long trip ... But not to China.

> **JOHNNY**
> What do you mean?

Duk Tang puts a portable iPod docking station on the table and
inserts an iPod into it. He presses the 'on' button.

> **NORMAN (VOICE ON IPOD)**
> *What are you worried about? We got away with murder.*

> **JOHNNY (VOICE ON IPOD)**
> *Yeah. You're right. Fuckin' murders. That's what we are. I
just wish this night was over. I hope that gun doesn't wash
up somewhere.*

NORMAN (VOICE ON IPOD)
That gun was a throwaway. Untraceable. Don't worry. The ocean swallowed up the evidence.

JOHNNY (VOICE ON IPOD)
Yeah. You're right. I'm just freaked out.

DUK TANG
(turns off the iPod)
Sounds like an airtight case to me ... Enough for a long trip to the penitentiary.

JOHNNY
That recording was doctored! ... Everything was taken out of context.

DUK TANG
Tell that to the FBI.

JOHNNY PUSHES BACK HARD WITH HIS CHAIR, and he ...

KNOCKS BOTH AH KAY AND XIN LIN BACKWARDS.

Johnny FAST-DRAWS HIS GUN. He ...

SHOOTS XIN LIN IN THE FOREHEAD.

Ah Kay points his GUN at Johnny.

PING JUMPS TO HER FEET, and ...

SHOOTS AH KAY SEVERAL TIMES IN THE CHEST.

Ah Kay topples onto his back; quite dead.

DUK TANG SPRINTS TOWARD THE STAIRS.

PING TACKLES DUK TANG.

She pulls Duk Tang to his feet.

Ping yanks a set of HANDCUFFS from inside her leather jacket and CUFFS DUK TANG'S HANDS BEHIND HIS BACK.

FOUR SWAT TEAM MEMBERS, aiming assault rifles, storm down the stairs.

Followed by FBI agents No. 1 and No. 2.

Ping hands Duk Tang over to the swat team.

The swat team pushes Duk Tang up the stairs.

> PING
> (to FBI AGENTS No. 1 & 2)
> Where were you guys? ... On spring break?

> FBI AGENT NO. 1
> Sorry, Agent O'Reilly ... We burst though the upstairs door as soon as we heard the first shots on the transmitter.

> JOHNNY
> Agent O'Reilly?

Ping takes her trademark Christian Dior eyeglasses out of her leather jacket and puts them on her face.

> PING
> Agent Ping O'Reilly .... Actually.

> JOHNNY
> (to FBI AGENTS NO. 1 and No. 2)
> You guys heard the shots over my transmitter? ... That's impossible! .... They smashed my Rolex to pieces.

PING
(shows Johnny her Rolex wristwatch)
I have one of those doohickeys too.

JOHNNY
My head is spinning here ... Could somebody please tell me what just happened?

FBI AGENT NO. 1
I'll leave that up to Agent O'Reilly ... You haven't been too nice to us lately.

JOHNNY
Not too nice? What did you want me to do? ... Take you guys to the senior prom?

FBI AGENT NO. 1
(pulls out his badge, shows it to Johnny)
Remember? ... F ... B ... I ... Famous But Incompetent.

JOHNNY
(laughs nervously)
I was just kidding ... Just a little joke of mine.

FBI AGENT NO. 1
You can take your jokes and shove them.

PING
(grabs Johnny's arm)
I'll explain every little detail; if you buy me dinner at Forlinis.

JOHNNY
Buy you dinner? ... You just saved my life! ... I'll buy you your own freakin' restaurant.

PING
Dinner will suffice.

FBI AGENT NO. 1
What about us? ... Don't we get dinner too?

JOHNNY
Sure. There's a nice little Chinese joint on Chatham
Square.
(beat)
But don't order the pork fried rice ... In fact, stay away
from the pork dishes altogether.

FBI AGENT NO. 1
Wiseguy.

JOHNNY
(to FBI AGENTS No 1 & No. 2)
Are either of you guys allergic to cats?

Ping grabs Johnny's arm and leads Johnny up the stairs.

INT. FORLINIS RESTAURANT - NIGHT

Johnny and Ping sit at a table in the back room of the restaurant. They are the only customers in the joint.

A busboy removes the soiled dinner dishes. A second busboy sweeps the crumbs off the table.

A waiter brings over a tray containing a bottle of Chivas Regal and two glasses. He places the tray on the table.

Johnny fills the two glasses with the Chivas Regal and he hands one glass to Ping.

> JOHNNY
> *(raises his glass)*
> Salute!

> PING
> *(raises her glass)*
> Bottoms up!

They both down the Chivas in one swallow.

> JOHNNY
> *(leans back in his chair)*
> Well, we both had a wild ride today ... Fill me in on the details that I obviously missed.

> PING
> Where should I start?

> JOHNNY
> How about at the beginning?

> PING
> Ok ... Years ago, when I was barely a teenager, the

Snakeheads smuggled me into New York City.

                    JOHNNY
          The Snakeheads ... Not the Facilitators?

                    PING
          Yes. The Snakeheads ... There were no Facilitators at the
time.

Ping pours them each a glass of Chivas Regal.

                    PING
                    (continues)
          My parents died when I was young. So my uncles in
          China gave the Snakeheads a $10,000 down payment to
          smuggle me into America ... The Land of Gold.

                    JOHNNY
          How much did your uncles owe the Snakeheads after you
arrived in America?

                    PING
          Another $40,000 ... But my uncles couldn't pay. And with
          the money I was making in the sweatshops, it would have
          taken me the rest of my life to settle the debt.
                    (beat)
          Then one day, I escaped.

                    JOHNNY
          What do you mean escaped?

                    PING
          It's a long story ... I rather keep that part a secret.

                    JOHNNY
          I know. Don't ask. Don't tell ... Sounds like the
          government's policy on the gays in the military.
                    (sips his scotch)
          Where did you go? You had no family here in America.

PING

I went straight to the police. I told them the truth about
me being in the country illegally. And I told them about
the Snakeheads ... Instead of deporting me, they brought
the FBI into the picture. The FBI placed me in a nice
foster home ... The O'Reillys took good care of me for
many years.

JOHNNY

Where are the O'Reillys now?

PING

They both passed away. First my mother.
    (beat)
She had a sudden heart attack ... No warning, no
nothing. I was devastated ... My father died nine months
later ... From a broken heart.

JOHNNY

Jesus, I'm sorry.

PING

Truth is, I have no family here in the United States. And
little I can remember in China.

Housie enters the back room of the restaurant. He paces slowly
to their table and kisses Ping's cheek.

Johnny stands. Housie bows slightly; then shakes Johnny's
hand.

JOHNNY
    (to Housie)
Have a seat. Can I get you a drink?

HOUSIE
(sits; points to the Chivas Regal)
Two fingers would be fine.

Johnny snatches a glass from an adjoining table and pours
Housie a short Chivas. Then he slouches back into this chair.

PING
(to Housie)
I was just telling Johnny the details of how I arrived in
America.

HOUSIE
(to Johnny)
Yes. Sister Ping went through some very hard times ...
But hard times make strong people.

PING
(to Johnny)
Now, tell me about you ... How long have you been
working undercover for the FBI?

JOHNNY

Not for the FBI ... With the FBI ... Those guys are jerks.

PING
(smiling)
Remember ... I'm FBI too.

JOHNNY
Right ... But you're different ... Obviously very different.
(sips scotch)
I started undercover right after I got promoted to
Detective ... Internal Affairs contacted me about working
in conjunction with the FBI to bring down the Chinese
gangs.

PING
So they partnered you with Norman Wong ... Who was
worse than most of the Chinese gang members.

JOHNNY
They figured Norman was up to something bad ... But they wanted more evidence linking him to more serious crimes.
(sips scotch)
I just didn't realized how bad he had gone.

HOUSIE
(stands)
Kids ... I must leave you now. I have very important business to attend to.

JOHNNY
(stands, shakes Housie's hand)
I guess I'll be seeing you around.

HOUSIE
Yes, you will.
(to Ping)
I came here tonight for a reason. Please see me first thing tomorrow morning. We have more work to do.

PING
I'll be there with bells on.

HOUSIE
(bows)
Goodbye to you both.

Housie exits the dining room.

JOHNNY
I'll make believe I didn't hear that.
(beat)
How about I pick you up for lunch tomorrow?

PING
(stands)
Great ... I'll meet you in my office at noon.

They kiss; passionately.

INT. CHINESE SOUP KITCHEN/OFFICE - DAY

Housie sits behind his desk; shuffling papers

We hear a KNOCK on the office door.

Housie stands. Like a man with a bad back, he shuffles to the door; peeks through the peephole, then opens the door.

Ping enters; carrying a SHOPPING BAG.

> PING
> *(kisses Housie's cheek)*
> Good morning, dear sir.

Housie sits behind his desk. He points to a chair on the opposite side of his desk.

> HOUSIE
> Please sit.
> *(smiles)*
> Or as they like to say in America 'Take a load off.'

Housie reaches into his desk drawer and removes a LARGE MANILA ENVELOPE. He hands the envelope across the desk to Ping.

> HOUSIE
> There's $30,000 in that envelope. I have three more people in China ready to escape ... Spread the money around where necessary ... If you need more money, come back to me.

Ping puts the manila envelope into her shopping bag.

> PING
> I have to check the flight schedules. I want to put the

three people on three different flights ... Just to be safe.

HOUSIE
You are doing good work, Sister Ping. The Chinese community is very proud of you ... I was afraid you were going to be transferred by the FBI out of Chinatown.

PING
Me too ... But I convinced my superiors that I can be more valuable here working undercover in Chinatown than I can sitting behind a desk somewhere else.

HOUSIE
There's still the Chinese gangs to deal with ... And the Tongs are presently deciding on Duk Tang's replacement.

PING
So I was right ... There is much more work for me to do.

HOUSIE
As always, be careful.

PING
As always, I will.

Ping stands; then exits the room.

INT. CHINATOWN TRAVEL AGENCY - DAY

Ping sits behind her desk. On the desk is the MANILA
ENVELOPE Housie gave her.

Johnny enters Ping's office.

Ping secretly slips the MANILA ENVELOPE into her desk
drawer.

> JOHNNY
>
> Hungry?

> PING
>
> I'm famished.

> JOHNNY
> *(shows Ping a brown paper bag)*
> I brought two sandwiches from Forlinis ... Meatball ...
And chicken parm.

> PING
>
> I'll take the meatball.

> JOHNNY
>
> Great. I'll take the chicken parm.

EXT. BAYARD STREET - DAY

Johnny and Ping stroll arm in arm through a dense lunchtime crowd. Johnny is carrying the paper bag filled with the sandwiches.

The sun is shining brightly. Birds are CHIRPING.

All is right with the world.

> JOHNNY
> I have two weeks off before Internal Affairs decides what to do with me ... How about you?

> PING
> I'm right back to work ... Places to go ... People to see ... Chinese to smuggle into America.
> *(smiling)*
> You know the drill.

> JOHNNY
> You can't even get a weekend off?

> PING
> Maybe ... But no more than a couple of days.

> JOHNNY
> We could go to Atlantic City for the weekend ... I have friends who can comp us.

> PING
> You forget. I own a travel agency ... I can get my own comps and mine are legal.

> JOHNNY
> We don't need separate rooms ... Do we?

> PING
> (*smiles*)
> Let me think about that.

Johnny stops and stares across the street.

JOHNNY'S P.O.V.

Paulie, dressed in his best mob suit, stands with his arms folded in a tenement entrance; acting like a bodyguard.

Vito stands opposite Paulie; his arm around a GORGEOUS CHINESE GIRL.

Paulie and Vito take turns whispering into each other's ear.

The gorgeous Chinese girl, a bored look on her face, reads a Chinese-American dictionary.

PAULIE'S P.O.V.

Paulie sees Johnny staring at him from across the street.

> PAULIE
> (*yells to Johnny*)
> Dinner at Mom's tonight?

BACK TO JOHNNY:

Johnny stares at Paulie for a second. Then with his thumb and forefinger, Johnny makes a shooting motion at Paulie.

Paulie feints horror and grabs his chest; like he's been shot.

Johnny smiles, then turns away from Paulie.

Johnny continues strolling down the street; arm-in-arm with Ping.

                    PING
          That's your brother? Isn't it?

                    JOHNNY
          Like they say ... You can pick your friends, but you can't
pick your relatives.
          (puts his arms around Ping's shoulder)
          Now what about the FBI? ... Are you getting a new
assignment?

                    PING
          No. The FBI is keeping me undercover in Chinatown. The
gangs are still a problem.

                    JOHNNY
          Good. That means we'll be seeing a lot more of each
other.

                    PING
               (smiles)
          We'll see about that.

Johnny and Ping stop walking. Johnny turns to Ping and holds
her in his arms.

                    JOHNNY
               (looks into Ping's eyes)
          Agent O'Reilly ... I think this is going to be the beginning
of a beautiful friendship.

                    PING
          Oh stop! This isn't Casablanca and you're no Humphrey
Bogart.

                    JOHNNY
               (imitates Bogart)
          Okay sweetheart. We'll cut right to the chase.

They kiss; passionately.

A DARK SEDAN SCREECHES TO A HALT in the middle of Bayard Street.

Ah Kay's girlfriend, LOIS, jumps out of the car.

Lois runs to where Johnny and Ping are standing.

Johnny and Ping turn towards Lois.

Lois aims a gun and ...

FIRES SEVERAL SHOTS AT PING.

Ping absorbs the shots in her stomach and chest. She slumps to the pavement.

Lois runs back to her car; slides inside the car and gets behind the wheel.

LOIS' CAR CAREENS DOWN BAYARD STREET; toward the Manhattan Bridge in the background.

Johnny drops the paper bag containing the sandwiches. He draws his gun from his shoulder holster, and SHOOTS at Lois' fleeing car; BLOWING OUT THE CAR'S BACK WINDOW.

Johnny dashes after Lois' car ...

REPEATEDLY FIRING HIS GUN.

Lois' car speeds towards the corner.

LOIS MAKES A WILD LEFT TURN; barely missing cars going north and south at the intersection of Bayard and the Bowery.

Lois' car disappears around the corner.

Johnny puts his gun back in his shoulder holster and sprints back to where Ping is lying in a **POOL OF BLOOD.**

Johnny kneels and sees Ping's unseeing eyes are wide open.

Johnny holds Ping's hand.

> **JOHNNY**
> *(tears flowing down both cheeks)*
> No, God! ... No!

Paulie and Vito kneel next to Johnny.

> **VITO**
> *(to Johnny)*
> She's gone kid.

> **JOHNNY**
> *(stands)*
> I'm going to hunt down that Chinese bitch and slice her to pieces.

A crowd of onlookers assembles and form a circle around Ping's body.

> **PAULIE**
> *(scans the crowd)*
> Easy, Johnny.
> *(nods towards the crowd)*
> We'll take care of this ourselves ... In due time.

> **JOHNNY**
> *(sobs on Paulie's shoulder)*
> I loved her, Paulie.

> **PAULIE**
> I know, Johnny ... I know.

SIREN BARING, AN AMBULANCE SCREECHES TO A HALT in the middle of Bayard Street.

TWO PARAMEDICS push through the crowd and rush toward Ping's body.

The paramedics bend down to administer to Ping.

They realize she is dead and they bow their heads in respect.

>   JOHNNY
>   (to Vito)
>   She didn't deserve this.

>   VITO
>   Forget it, kid... Things like this happen around here ... It's
>   Chinatown.
>   (beat)
>   This won't go unpunished ... You have my word on that.
>   (beat)
>   My solemn word.

Paulie puts his arm around Johnny's shoulder and leads Johnny away from Ping's body. Vito follows close behind.

Suddenly, Vito turns towards the crowd. His mouth twists into a snarl and tears fall down both cheeks.

>   VITO
>   (to the crowd)
>   Go home! ... The show is over! ... Go the fuck home!
>   (beat)
>   I'll take care of this.

The crowd quickly disperses in all directions.

Vito turns and strides quickly towards Johnny and Paulie, who are walking slowly with their backs to him.

Paulie has his arm around Johnny's slumped shoulder.

The three men totter slowly out of the picture.

CLOSE ON - CORNER STREET SIGN, which is written in both English and in Chinese:

"MOTT & BAYARD."

FADE OUT:

As usual, I am eager to hear comments from all my readers; may they be negative or positive. I enjoy discovering that a reader enjoys one of my books, but I sometimes learn more from critical comments.

My email address is: jbruno999@aol.com.

So fire away!

Bonus Feature!

The Cotton Club

THE BLACKS WERE ON THE STAGE.
THE WHITES WERE AT THE TABLES.
THE MOBSTERS WERE BEHIND THE SCENES.
AND SOMEHOW THE MAGIC TOUCHED THEM ALL
– Jim Haskins - "The Cotton Club."

In the 1890s, Harlem was a land speculator's dream. The elevated railroad lines that had been extended to 129th Street in Manhattan had transformed the area from the hinterlands to what was called "The Great Migration."

At the time, black families lived mostly in the area between 37th and 58th Streets, between Eighth and Ninth Avenues. The upper crust of society viewed Harlem as the next step for the upwardly mobile, and as a result, splendorous townhouses costing thousands more than comparables downtown were being built as fast as the Harlem land could be purchased by speculators.

By 1905, however, the Harlem real estate market dropped through the floor. Land speculators were forced to face the fact that the townhouses had been built too quickly and the prices were far above what people were prepared to pay.

On the verge of bankruptcy, the land speculators used tactics that today would be illegal. They rented their buildings to black tenants, far above what they would charge white tenants. Then, in a frenzy to recapture their losses, the land speculators approached white building owners, and they told them if they didn't purchase their vacant buildings they would rent them out exclusively to blacks, thereby reducing the value of the white landowner's properties.

The white landowners didn't bite, so the land speculators made good on their promises. Whites began moving out of Harlem in droves, replaced by black families who had never lived in such a fine neighborhood. Black churches followed their congregations from the slums of Manhattan to the splendor of Harlem, and by the early 1920s, Harlem was the largest black community in the United States.

However, most blacks could not afford the high rents charged by the white building owners, so they took in tenants, resulting in two and sometimes three families living in a one, or two-bedroom apartment. Coinciding with the overcrowding of Harlem, came the influx of illegal enterprises, such as numbers running, houses of prostitution, and drug dealers. This was counteracted somewhat when prosperous blacks, mostly in the entertainment business, decided Harlem was where they could showcase their talents in a neighborhood filled with people of their own race.

Fritz Pollard, noted All-American football player, who made his money in real estate, moved to Harlem, as did fellow All-American football player Paul Robeson; destined to hone an outstanding career acting and singing on stage. They were quickly followed by famous singers like Ethel Walters and Florence Mills, and Harlem was ready for a renaissance equal to that of the glowing White Way on Broadway.

However, where there was money to be made, white gangsters like Dutch Schultz and Owney "The Killer" Madden were ready to jump in and take the profits; by force if necessary. Schultz muscled his way into the Harlem numbers business, chasing out such black notables as Madam Stephanie St. Claire and Caspar Holstein. During the height of Prohibition, Madden had his eyes on the perfect place to sell his bootleg booze: The *Club Deluxe* on 142nd Street and Lenox Avenue.

The *Club Deluxe* was owned by former world heavyweight champion Jack Johnson, the first black heavyweight champion of the world. Whereas, Johnson was proficient with his fists, Madden and his formidable crew were good with guns, knives, and bats. A few choice words, backed up with the threat of violence and few meager bucks thrown in, forced Johnson to hand over *Club Deluxe* to Madden and his partner/manager George "Big Frenchy" DeMange. The two gangsters renamed it *The Cotton Club*.

Not to totally insult a black man of Johnson's stature, Madden threw Johnson a bone. Madden allowed Johnson to hang around the joint, showcasing his black tuxedo and a toothy smile. Johnson told customers he was the assistant manager of *The Cotton Club* under

DeMange, but that was not true and just a way for Johnson to save face.

To understand why such a great heavyweight boxer like Johnson would cower before Madden, who was barely five-foot-five-inches and 140 pounds after a huge dinner, one would have to understand Madden's background.

Owen "Owney" Madden was born at 25 Somerset Street, in Leeds, England, on December 18, 1891. In need of work, his father moved the Madden family to Liverpool. In 1903, when young Madden was only 12, his father died and his mother re-located her family to America, settling on the West Side of Manhattan in a neighborhood called "Hell's Kitchen."

Madden fell in with a boisterous gang known as the Gophers (pronounced Goo-fers). He became proficient in the favored crimes of the era: robberies, muggings, and labor racket beatings. In order to hurt and intimidate, Madden's favorite weapon was a lead pipe wrapped in newspaper.

Madden made tons of money in a racket called the "insurance business." As the president of his own "insurance company," Madden would visit the local establishments and tell the business owners that they needed "bomb insurance," in case foreigners (Madden himself) decided to bomb the businessman's store. The business owners understood the implications, and they paid Madden plenty.

If a foolhardy business owner snubbed Madden, that man's store would go up in flames within 24 hours and sometimes even minutes of their refusal to pay. While Madden was a member of the Gophers and making lots of dough in his "insurance business," he was arrested 44 times, but not once was he sent to prison.

When Madden was 17, he earned his nickname "The Killer." A poor Italian immigrant did nothing wrong, except to cross paths with Madden on a street in Hell's Kitchen. In front of a crowd of his fellow Gophers and whomever else was standing on the street that day, Madden pulled out a gun, and he shot the Italian dead.

Then Madden stood over the dead body, and he announced to the assembled crowd, "I'm Owney Madden!"

By the time he was 23, Madden had at least five other murders to his credit. Hence the nickname - "The Killer."

However, Madden thought he was bulletproof, until November

6, 1912, when he ventured into the Arbor Dance Hall, which was located in the heart of the territory controlled by the Gopher's rivals: the Hudson Dusters. Like he had nary a care in the world, Madden strolled into the hall by himself during a dance given by the Dave Hyson Association.

Madden was watching the proceedings from the balcony, when 11 Hudson Dusters surrounded him and shot Madden six times. Madden was rushed to the hospital, where a detective asked Madden who had done the dirty deed.

"Nothin' doin,'" Madden said. "It's no business but mine who put these slugs into me. My boys will get them."

By the time Madden was released from the hospital, six of his 11 assailants had already been shot dead.

While Madden was recuperating from his wounds, one of his fellow Gophers, Little Patsy Doyle, figured he'd take control of Madden's gang. Doyle was also intent on taking back his former girlfriend, Freda Horner, who now was the sole property of Owney Madden. Miss Horner told Madden about Doyle's intentions, and as a result, Madden told Miss Horner to inform Doyle she would be glad to meet him for a date at a saloon on Eighth Avenue and 41st Street. When Doyle arrived, dressed to the nines and all smiles, two of Madden's gunmen shot Doyle dead.

Being the obvious suspect, Madden was arrested three days later for the murder of Little Patsy Doyle. At Madden's trial, he was shocked to discover that Miss Horner had betrayed him, too. Miss Horner testified in court that it was Madden who had set up the Doyle murder. As a result, Madden was convicted and sentenced to 10-20 years in Sing Sing Prison. He did only eight years and was released in 1923, just in time to strong-arm Jack Johnson into selling him the *Club Deluxe*, a.k.a.— *The Cotton Club*.

By this time Madden was big into bootlegging with his partner Big Bill Dwyer, and *The Cotton Club* was the perfect place to sell their illegal hooch, especially Madden's No. 1 beer, which was considered the best brew in New York City. They took in a legitimate guy named Herman Stark as their front man/partner/stage manager, but the show within the show was completely run by Madden and DeMange.

According to Jim Haskins's book *The Cotton Club*, when Madden and DeMange took over the joint they redid the entire interior "to cater to the white downtowner's taste for the primitive." The club was made over in "jungle decor," with numerous artificial palm trees dotted throughout the spacious establishment, which had seating for 700 people. The most exquisite draperies, tablecloths, and fixtures were purchased, indicating this was a "plush late-night supper club," and the exorbitant prices highlighted that fact. The menu was varied. Besides the traditional steaks and chops, *The Cotton Club* cooks drummed up Chinese and Mexican dishes, as well as "Harlem" cuisine like fried chicken and barbecued spareribs.

DeMange presided over the front door like a tyrant. One rule was perfectly clear. Although the waiters, busboys, bartenders, cooks, service personnel, and performers were all black, no black people were allowed inside as customers. (The name itself – *The Cotton Club* -- came from the light brown color of undyed cotton.)

The chorus girls had to be "tall, tan, and terrific," which meant they had to be at least 5-feet-6-inches tall, light-skinned and no older than 21. The girls also had to be expert dancers and at least be able to carry a tune. For some unknown reason, there was no color-shade restriction on the black male dancers, who were all proficient in "high-stepping, gyrating and snake-dancing."

To show how strict Madden and DeMange were about their policy of segregation, about a month before their second grand opening *(The Cotton Club* was closed by Prohibition agents for a while, even though the local cops were on the pad), the following job interview took place. Present were Madden and DeMange, along with their choreographer Althea Fuller and their orchestra conductor Andy Preer. The girl being interviewed was Queenie Duchamp.

DeMange to Madden: Boss, when is the club going to be ready to open?

Madden: The pigs won't cause us trouble for a time. They know if we're forced to close for bootlegging they won't get their bonuses. As it is, they're missing the extra padding and the boys have been complaining to the Sarge. Yeah, they've learned their lesson. As for the club's show... let's ask Althea and Andy.

DeMange to Preer: Andy, how's the pit? Ready for next month's opening?

Preer: We will be. If Althea gets her girls ready, the pit is ready to stomp.

Althea Fuller: Boss, we had a setback. One of the girls went and found a "moral conscience." She's following her sister, a Garveyite, back to Africa. Shame, she was a looker in the front line. Don't worry, Boss, I've already got replacements ready to audition for you today. One of them looks promising and comes with a recommendation. She's in the front row, third one in ... Queenie Duchamp. First, let's see if she can remember the steps she was taught this morning.

(Andy Preer leads the orchestra in "I've Found a New Baby" and five dancing girls audition. Queenie Duchamp is third from the left.)

Madden: Keep the third and the fifth. The other girls are too dark and short. Althea, make sure you grill them about rules and rehearsals. We are NOT running a gut bucket operation here.

(Madden leaves with his bodyguards)

Fuller: Queenie, come here. You got the job on a few conditions.

Queenie: Anything you want Miss Fuller.

Fuller: Number one - No booze, No boys, No drugs. No exceptions.

Queenie: Yes, Miss.

Fuller: Number two- Rehearsals are Tuesday, Wednesday, Thursday, and Friday starting at 1 p.m. sharp. All rehearsals are MANDATORY and lateness will not be accepted. I don't know what you've heard, but rehearsals here are grueling and performances are long with many elaborate costume changes. That means you can't afford to be draggin' your ass around here. Make sure you eat and get your rest. Do you understand?

Queenie: Yes, Miss Fuller.

Fuller: Number three - No mixing with the patrons. There are about 700 whitefolk that walk through those doors every night. And according to Mr. Madden, they only have one goal here and that's to spend money. They come here to hear the best Negro music and dance numbers in the city. They might act like they want to be your friend after a couple of drinks, but they don't. Mr. Madden doesn't want the races mixin', and as far as I'm concerned, I think that's better for business anyway.

DeMange: If a white customer starts to give you a problem or tries to make a connection with you, tell me. I'll take care of it. It's happened before. Sometimes these rich people get a couple drinks in them, and they think they own the world. Don't worry about it, just let me know. We run a tight ship here.

Queenie: Yes, Mr. DeMange. No problem Ms. Fuller. I am an entertainer and I understand the importance of practice. In fact, I'm a singer, a blues singer! If you ever need a singer ..... (Ms. Fuller and Mr. DeMange look at each other.)

Fuller: Look, missy. Your goal here is to dance, smile, and follow the rules... not sing. Got it?

Queenie: Yes, Miss Fuller. Got it.

Fuller: Another thing... stay out of trouble. You're a looker, and the club world can be dirty and dangerous. It doesn't have to be though. Keep to yourself and whatever you do, stay out of Mr. Madden's way. If you do this, you'll be fine. Now go to wardrobe for a fitting.

Queenie: Yes and thank you, Miss Fuller.

The Cotton Club was an immediate success with the downtown swells. On opening night, the Fletcher Henderson band entertained the crowd (Henderson's band was the house band until June 1931). Through radio broadcasts originating nightly from *The Cotton Club,* Henderson's band was such a success, he became one of the most sought-after band leaders in America. Following Henderson was the Duke Ellington Band (until 1934), and then Cab Calloway and the Cotton Club Orchestra.

Despite the fact the only booze served on the premises was Madden's No. 1 beer, customers were allowed, and even encouraged to bring their own booze that they had obtained illegally elsewhere. Of course, the management had a hefty set-up charge, which included the glasses, ice, and the mixers.

If a customer came unprepared and still wanted booze instead of beer, the doorman, and sometimes even a waiter, came in handy. A bottle of champagne would cost a customer $30, and a bottle of scotch cost $18; a kingly sum in those days. But the customers were well-healed, and nobody ever griped about the prices; at least nobody who cared about their continued good health.

After a while, DeMange and Madden lightened up a bit on the "no-black-customers-allowed" policy. This happened in 1932, right after W.C. Handy, known as "The King of the Blues," was denied admission, even though the Duke Ellington Band was inside playing songs that Handy had written himself. Ellington pleaded his case to Madden, and Madden agreed to loosen his policy. But just a little bit.

Light-skinned blacks were now allowed in as customers, as well as a few darker blacks who were famous entertainers themselves. However, blacks in mixed parties was a definite no-no.

Writer and photographer Carl Van Vechten wrote, "There were brutes at the front door to enforce *The Cotton Club's* policy which was opposed to mixed parties."

Jim Haskins wrote in *The Cotton Club*, "Only the lightest-complexioned Negroes gained entrance, and even they were carefully screened. The club's management was aware that most white downtowners wanted to *observe* Harlem blacks, not with mix with them."

Even famed comedian Jimmy Durante displayed blatant racism when he said, "It isn't necessary to mix with colored people if you don't feel like it. You have your own party and keep to yourself. But it's worth seeing. How they step!"

Durante went as far as to intimate that blacks were innately more violent than whites.

"Racial lines are drawn here to prevent possible trouble," Durante said. "Nobody wants razors, blackjacks, or fists flying. And the chances of war are less if there's no mixing."

Madden and DeMange, and *The Cotton Club*, suffered a little setback, when on July 15 , 1931, Irish hoodlum Vincent "Mad Dog" Coll saw how much cash *The Cotton Club* was raking in, and he decided to take a piece of the action for himself. Coll did this by brazenly kidnapping DeMange and holding him for ransom. Madden forked over $35,000 to Coll to get his partner/manager back, but there was no satisfying Coll. Even knowing that Madden had put a $50,000 bounty on Coll's head, in March of 1932, Coll, hiding from the police (and Madden) and desperate for money, phoned Madden and demanded $100,000 *not* to kidnap Madden.

Coll, who was holed up in the Cornish Arms Hotel on West 23rd Street with his wife, Lottie, told Madden, "Imagine how the Dagos and Kikes is gonna feel when they have to shell out a hundred grand to save your sorry ass. Pay me now, up front, and I'll save you the trouble."

A broad smile on his face, Madden told Coll he'd think about it.

Madden knew this was the perfect opportunity to get rid of Coll and his kidnappings, once and for all.

On March 8, 1932, Madden phoned Coll, and he told Coll to call him from the phone booth at the New London Pharmacy, across the street from Cornish Arms and he'd make arrangement for the hundred grand to be delivered to Coll. While Coll was in the drug store phone booth in the back speaking on the phone with Madden, a man with a machine gun hidden under his long coat, calmly walked up to Coll and emptied 15 rounds into Coll, making Madden and DeMange happy and relieved, to say the least.

In 1933, after he settled a little problem with the IRS and with Prohibition repealed, Madden decided to call it a day. He handed over the reins of *The Cotton Club* to DeMange, and he hightailed it to Hot Springs, Ark., where he opened a hotel/spa, which became the favorite hideout for New York mobsters on the lam from the law. In fact, when New York Mafioso Lucky Luciano was in hiding, because a bulldog special prosecutor named Thomas E. Dewey had a warrant for Luciano's arrest on a trumped-up prostitution charge, it was at Madden's resort where Luciano was finally arrested after four months on the run.

Of course, Madden was still a silent partner with DeMange in *The Cotton Club*, but the huge profits would soon diminish, before coming completely to a halt in Harlem.

It started with the Great Depression, which had cut down dramatically on the disposable income of the rich, and the formerly rich. Downtown revelers who had frequented *The Cotton Club* came less often, and when they did come, they spent less money. These same revelers got caught up in the street gang mentality, and as a result, an avalanche of bullets started flying in Harlem; whites shooting blacks, blacks shooting whites, and members of the same race slinging shots at each other. With so much lead zinging though the Harlem air, white-oriented Harlem clubs like *The Cotton Club* suffered a dramatic decrease in attendance.

In addition, no area of America was affected more by the Depression than Harlem. By 1934, according to the New York Urban League, more than 80 percent of Harlem residents were on "Home Relief," which we now call "Welfare." The Reverend Adam Clayton Powell fanned the flames of racial tensions when he started leading boycotts of white-owned stores in Harlem, in order to force them to hire more black workers. Despair and resentment sprung up in the streets of Harlem, and this led to a fateful day in Harlem history.

A dark-skinned, 16-year-old Puerto Rican named Lino Rivera was sulking around the streets of Harlem, out of work and desperately looking for a job; any job. To pass the time, he took in a movie, and then went to the Kress Department Store on 125th Street. There he spotted a knife he wanted, but the knife cost 10 cents and Rivera didn't have 10 cents.

Rivera had just snatched the knife and put it into his pocket, when a male employee of the store grabbed Rivera, and a scuffle ensued. While the two men were battling, another white employee jumped in and tried to help subdue Rivera. In seconds, a crowd of black shoppers surrounded the fight, obviously favoring Rivera. During the melee, Rivera bit the thumb of one of the white employees.

The injured man shouted, "I'm going to take you down to the basement and beat the hell out of you."

Within minutes, the rumor had spread around the streets of Harlem that two white men were beating a black boy to death. This false rumor received dubious confirmation, when a blaring ambulance pulled up in front of the Kress Department Store. It made no difference the ambulance was there for the white man who had the severely bitten finger.

That night the streets of Harlem erupted in bedlam. Born out of resentment of the Depression, and the dismal way white people had been treating black people in Harlem for years, hundreds of blacks rioted in the streets. They looted white-owned stores, and they pilfered merchandise as if it was their own.

The perception of the downtown whites was that Harlem was no longer safe for them to venture into, even to see the wondrous entertainment at *The Cotton Club*. In addition, black musicians and entertainers no longer considered *The Cotton Club* as the top of the heap. It became a place where the entertainers could start their careers, but once they got noticed, they went on to bigger and better things. Business became so bad at *The Cotton Club* (and other Harlem nightclubs that catered to the white downtown crowd, such as *Small's Paradise* on 7th Avenue), Harlem's *The Cotton Club* closed its doors for good on February 16, 1936.

DeMange and Herman Stark, with Madden's blessing from Hot Springs, moved *The Cotton Club* downtown to 48th Street and Broadway, to a space formerly occupied by *The Harlem Club*. The new *Cotton Club* was an immediate success. It had its grand re-opening on September 24, 1936. Cab Calloway and Bill "Bojangles" Robinson performed that night, as did Avis Andrews, the Berry Brothers, and the gorgeous Katherine Perry, who was so light-skinned she could easily pass for being white.

Because it was so accessible with its new Midtown location, *The Cotton Club* was raking in the cash. In the third week alone, it grossed more than $45,000, and in the first 16 weeks, the average weekly gross was $30,000.

The prices in the new joint were higher than *The Cotton Club's* in Harlem. A steak sandwich rose from $1.25 to $2.25. Scrambled eggs with Deerfield sausage rose from $1.25 to a $1.50 and lobster cocktails went from $1.00 to $1.50.

Still DeMange and Stark kept packing them in.

One price that did decrease was *The Cotton Club's* cover charge. In Harlem, in order to keep the "undesirables" away, the cover charge was $3 per table. However, since blacks very rarely crossed the "Mason-Dixon Line" of 110th Street, *The Cotton Club's* cover charge was $2 per table during dinner time, and nothing after that.

The Cotton Club continued to thrive until the summer of 1939, when the Internal Revenue Service served the club's management with indictments for income tax evasion. The indictments hit the Cotton Club Management Corporation, including Herman Stark, president, George Goodrich, accountant, and Noah Braustein, secretary-treasurer, with four counts of failure to pay and embezzlement of taxes. If convicted, all three men faced up to 25 years in prison, and fines of up to $20,000 apiece. Amazingly, because he was just listed as an employee, Frenchy DeMange escaped the indictment. At trial, the Cotton Club Management Corporation was found guilty, but the three officers escaped conviction. Still, Stark had to fork over a hefty fine to the government, in addition to $3,400 owed in back taxes.

At the start of 1940, it was obvious that *The Cotton Club*, and Herman Stark, had money problems. Besides the high midtown rent and the effects of the Depression, the unions, especially the musician union, had a stranglehold on Stark and his profits. Before his problems with the I.R.S., Stark was skimming money off the top to make up for any shortfalls the unions and the high entertainment payrolls caused. But with the government watching *The Cotton Club* like a hawk, skimming was now impossible.

The Cotton Club closed its door for good on June 10, 1940. Stark and DeMange gave no official reason, but as one columnist put it, the main reason was, "the lack of the famous, old filthy lucre."

Yet, that explanation would be too simplistic. Of course, money was a problem, but also America's taste for music like Duke Ellington's and Cab Calloway's was changing too. The younger generation of Americans was enthralled with the new jazz and "swing" styles of white bandleaders like Tommy Dorsey, Artie Shaw, and the "King of Swing," Benny Goodman.

The Cotton Club was a great idea whose life span had run its course. The black entertainers who had cut their teeth working at *The Cotton Club*, people like Duke Ellington, Cab Calloway, Louis Armstrong, Ella Fitzgerald, and Lena Horne, all went on to establish long and wondrous careers. But the concept of a nightclub with all black entertainment no longer appealed to the white mainstream of America.

The Cotton Club closed because it was a concept that had blossomed, then like a gilded rose, slowly withered away. Still, the impact of *The Cotton Club* on society will linger for as long as song and dance remains an integral part of our American culture.

*****

Second Bonus Feature!

Satan's Circus

At the end of the Civil War, New York City was a den of iniquity, with prostitution as common as warm beer in a cold dive.

Although flesh-peddling was available on the Lower East and West Sides of Manhattan, the most prolific area of prostitution was called Satan's Circus, which was the area between 24th and 40th Streets, and between Fifth and Seventh Avenues. The "Main Street" of Satan's Circus was Broadway between 23rd and 42nd Streets, which was then known as "The Line." Satan's Circus later became part of a larger tract of decadence known as "The Tenderloin," which was also infamous for its grifters and numerous gambling dens.

In the 1890s, after Tom Edison electrified New York City, that stretch of Broadway in the Tenderloin, because of the numerous lighted advertising signs prominent on the streets, was called "The Great White Way." In the early 1900s, when the theater district moved uptown, the "Great White Way's" name was conveyed to the area on Broadway above Times Square.

After the Civil War, the New York City police were greatly demoralized; destroyed by corruption within their own ranks and by a Tammany Hall political system that reeked of graft. As a result, the police spent very little time actually policing Satan's Circus. In fact, there is great evidence that the police themselves profited from the prostitution houses by getting weekly cuts from the proceeds.

John A. Kennedy, the Superintendent of Police in New York City, was one of the few New York City cops not on the take. During the Civil War Riots of 1863, Kennedy was almost beaten to death when he tried to step in and personally stop the riots. The angry crowd descended upon Kennedy, pummeling him unmercifully. Kennedy was saved only because a sympathetic passerby witnessed his beating and told the angry crowd that Kennedy was already dead.

Kennedy tried as hard as he could to diminish the bordello epidemic in Satan's Circus, but he was overwhelmed by the noncooperation of his cops and by the direct intervention of the powers that be at Tammany Hall. The simple fact was, as soon as Kennedy ordered a bordello closed and its occupants arrested, the dirty politicians stepped in. The very next day, the bordello was back open and its employees dutifully back at work.

In 1866, Kennedy released a report to Bishop Simpson of the Methodist Episcopal Church, who lorded over 20,000 parishioners. Bishop Simpson had made a sermon in which he said there were more prostitutes in New York City than he had parishioners. Kennedy rebutted Bishop Simpson's statement by saying his police records showed that there were "3,300 prostitutes in New York City, working in 621 bordellos and 99 hotels. This figure also included 747 waiter girls employed in concert saloons and dance halls."

Bishop Simpson chided Kennedy over his report, saying Kennedy was not considering the thousands of "street walkers" who frequented dive bars and stalked the streets of New York City during the dimly lit night hours. Reverend Thomas De Witt Talmage, who was on a mission to end the sins of Satan's Circus, called the entire city of New York "the modern Gomorrah" for allowing Satan's Circus to exist.

In the 1860s, the most famous of the bordellos in Satan's Circus was called Sisters' Row, which was located at 25th Street near Seventh Avenue. Sisters' Row was a series of seven side-by-side brothels run by seven sisters, who had come to New York City from a New England village seeking fame and fortune. At first, the seven sisters tried to get legitimate jobs, but then they realized that the sex trade was rampant, out in the open, protected by the police, and quite profitable. So why not make some serious money from this phenomenon?

Sisters' Row was considered the most expensive bordello in New York City. It was frequented by the blue-bloods of society, and quite frankly, only the rich could afford the prices. The working girls were advertised as "cultured and pleasing companions, accomplished on the piano and guitar, and familiar with the charms and graces of correct sexual intercourse."

On certain days of the month, no man was admitted unless he had an engraved invitation, wore evening dress, and carried a bouquet of flowers. And on Christmas Eve, all the proceeds garnered that night on Sisters' Row was donated to charity.

By 1885, police estimated that half the buildings in Satan's Circus were dedicated to some form of deviant behavior. Sixth Avenue itself was teeming with brothels, dives, and all-night saloons. Plus, the streets were packed with seedy customers looking for a few bright moments in their otherwise dull lives.

Satan's Circus and the entire Tenderloin district were the responsibility of the 29th Precinct, whose jurisdiction ran from 14th Street to 42nd Street, and from Fourth to Seventh Avenues. In 1876, Captain Alexander "Clubber" Williams was transferred to the 29th Precinct to be its leader. Williams, the exact opposite of Kennedy in terms of honesty, was quite pleased with his transfer.

Williams told a pal, "Well, I've been transferred. I've had nothing but chuck steak for a while, and now I'm going to get me a little of the tenderloin."

One of the most famous joints in Satan's Circus was the Haymarket, on Sixth Avenue between 29th and 30th streets. The Haymarket originally opened right after the Civil War as an opera house and was named after a similar playhouse in London, England. But The Haymarket could not compete with the more established playhouses like the Trivoli Theater and Tony Pastor's, so it closed in 1878.

Soon after, the Haymarket was renovated and re-opened as a dancehall. But it was actually a dancehall in only the very restrictive sense of the word. Quite frankly, the Haymarket became a three-story, yellow brick den of iniquity. It was a hunting ground for prostitutes, thugs, and pickpockets who preyed mostly on out-of-town yokels, who had heard of the infamous Haymarket and wanted to experience its storied vices. The Haymarket reached the height of its fame in New York City's Gilded Age of the 1880s and 1890s, and after enduring several closings, the Haymarket remained open, in one form or the other, until 1913.

Woman at the Haymarket were admitted at no charge. However, men were obliged to pay a 25-cent admission fee, which allowed them to buy cheap drinks, dance, and carouse with the young ladies, the vast majority of whom were cheap prostitutes. In addition to a huge bar, all three floors of the Haymarket contained little private cubicles, where raunchy woman gave their marks a cheap rendition of the cancan, and for a few bucks more they turned these cubicles into a New York City version of the French peep shows. One can imagine what a few bucks more might have enticed these women to do, and do quickly, so that they could move on to their next customer.

The real action came well after midnight, when the Haymarket's floors were littered with drunken revelers, some of whom were barely conscious. That's when the muggers and pickpockets sprang into action, leaving the poor men, again, most of them out-of-towners, with no loose change in their pockets to make their way back home.

If you wanted to see a bearded lady with a bat, the place to go in Satan's Circus was the French Madame's on 31st Street just off Sixth Avenue. The place was named after its owner, a big bruiser of a broad who had a five o'clock shadow all day long and every day of the week. This female moose sat on a high stool near the cash register, and if a young lady was making too much noise, or making a fool of herself, the French Madame would clock her on the head with a bludgeon and then fling the young lady out into the street by her hair.

The main room of the French Madame's looked like a dining room, but in fact, no food was served there except black coffee. The booze flowed freely, and there were small cubicles on the second floor where women, young and old, pretty and pretty-ugly, danced the cancan for anyone who cared to watch. For a buck, a young lady would dance in the nude, and for an additional fee, who knows what else transpired in those small private cubicles.

If someone wanted an alcoholic beverage mixed by the best bartender in town, the place to go in Satan's Circus was the Star and Garter, located at Sixth Avenue and 30th Street, owned by Ed Coffee, a renowned sportsman of his time. Coffee employed Billy Patterson, who was generally thought of as the best darn mixer-of-drinks in all of New York City. Billy made a mean martini, but he also was an expert in creating exotic mixtures, containing two more types of liquors; which if you asked for these same drinks in virtually any other ginmill in town, you would have been thrown out by the scruff of your neck.

A sign stating "Booze or beer, or get the heck out of here" was the norm in virtually every dive in New York City, but not at the Star and Garter.

Patterson was such a jovial fellow, and he made so many people happy with his drink concoctions, it was thought that Patterson didn't have an enemy in the world. But apparently that was not the case. One day as Patterson left the Star and Garter by a side entrance, someone clocked him in the side of the head with a rock slung from a slingshot. The assailant was never found, but the phrase "Who Struck Billy Patterson?" resounded throughout the streets of Satan's Circus for many days to come.

After a while, that phrase took on a life of its own. It was uttered whenever people were mystified about anything.

"Who Struck Billy Patterson?" was uttered when somebody robbed a cash register, or if a favored sports team was somehow beaten by a rank underdog. "Who Struck Billy Patterson?" was also exclaimed when someone, who was one day very poor, somehow came into some cash, by legitimate, or illegitimate means.

Another popular Satan's Circus hotspot was the Cremorne, located in the basement of a building on 32nd Street between Sixth and Seventh Avenues. The owner of the Cremorne, which was said to have been named after a British tavern, was an overbearing dolt known only as Don Whiskerandos. The Don was a whale-shaped man with a huge beard and a walrus-type mustache, which ran down both sides of his bloated face. Don Whiskerandos's mission in life was to ensure the scantily clad ladies, whom he employed, made certain the men who staggered inside his dive bought the ladies drinks at inflated prices.

Men's drinks cost 15 cents or two for a quarter. But ladies drinks cost a whopping 20 cents, of which the ladies were paid a small commission by Don Whiskerandos.

Every time a sap bought a lady a drink, the lady received a small brass check to keep a tally on what she was owed at the end of the night. And if a sucker sprang for a bottle of wine for the lady, she kept the cork as proof of purchase.

Next door to the Cremorne was an establishment with the same name. It was not a drinking joint, nor a place where a man might pick up a chick. It was, in fact, a mission run by a former alcoholic named Jerry McAuley.

Quite often, and always by accident, some lad looking for a good time would wander into the wrong Cremorne. When this happened, McAuley sprang into action. He quickly locked the door behind the befuddled chap. Then after plying him with sandwiches and coffee as thick as mud, McAuley would launch into a mighty sermon on the wages of sin caused by the excesses of alcohol.

Needless to say, McAuley and Don Whiskerandos were not the best of pals, since The Don blamed McAuley for any shortages in The Don's daily cash register receipts.

Other noted dives in Satan's Circus were Egyptian Hall on 34th street between Fifth and Sixth Avenues; Sailor's Hall on 30th Street (which was mostly frequented by Negroes); Buckingham Palace on 27th Street, which was famous for its masked balls, and Tom Gould's on 31st Street, which was basically a large saloon with rooms for rent upstairs, rented by the day and sometimes even by the hour.

By the turn of the 20th century, Satan's Circus was in steady decline. The advent of the Ladies Temperance Movement and the stalwart work of people like Carrie Nation and the Reverend Charles H. Parkhurst, prompted the New York City police to crack down on the vices being perpetrated in Satan's Circus.

In 1895, Mayor Strong appointed Teddy Roosevelt as Police Commissioner of New York City. Roosevelt went hard after crooked cops who were taking pieces of the pie from the dives in Satan's Circus. Soon, places that were teeming with sex and sexual innuendo were the exception and not the rule in the area between 24th and 40th Streets, and between Fifth and Seventh Avenues.

After the police crackdown in Satan's Circus, drinking establishments still abounded in all parts of New York City. But bawdy play and sex-for-pay was moved from out in the open to behind closed doors, where, of course, they remain to this very day.

As much as things change, sometimes they still remain the same.

Third Bonus Feature!

Typhoid Mary Mallon

She was an ignorant, ill-tempered woman, but an excellent cook. However, Typhoid Mary Mallon's refusal to accept the fact she was a healthy carrier of the deadly typhoid bacteria helped cause the deaths of at least three people.

Mary Mallon was born in 1869 in Cookstown, County Tyrone, Ireland (now Northern Ireland). She immigrated to America in 1884 and worked in a succession of menial jobs, until she discovered she had an exceptional talent as a cook (it was reported she made a delicious peach ice cream).

No one knows when the anomaly occurred, but sometime in the early 20th century, Mary became a healthy carrier of the typhoid bacterium (Salmonella typhi). Mary never got sick herself, so it was beyond her comprehension (or maybe she didn't want to believe it was possible) that she was a monumental cause of extreme physical distress to other people, who just happened to come into contact with her while she worked at her cooking profession. (Washing her hands properly before cooking and serving food wouldn't have hurt much either.)

Typhoid fever is a world-wide bacterial disease "transmitted by the ingestion of food or water contaminated with the feces of an infected person, containing the bacterium Salmonella enterica, serovar Typhi." The bacteria then penetrates though the infected person's intestinal walls into their blood stream. The symptoms of an infected person include high fever, diarrhea, and gastroenteritis. If not treated properly, the fever can last up to four weeks and sometimes ends with the infected person experiencing delirium, before finally dying. A person may become an asymptomatic carrier (suffering no symptoms themselves) of the typhoid bacteria, and five percent of the people infected continue to carry the disease after they recover.

The World Health Organization estimated that through the years 1906-1960 there were anywhere from 16-33 million cases of typhoid fever worldwide, with 216,000 of them resulting in fatalities. The age group with the highest incidence of infection were children and teenagers between the ages of 5-19.

In the time period of around 434-430 BC, it is believed that typhoid fever killed one-third of the population of Athens, Greece, including Greek leader Pericles. During this period, the entire population of the peninsula of Attica was quarantined within the Long Walls, and they lived in tents.

Historians believe that in the English colony of Jamestown, Virginia, between 1607 and 1624, typhoid fever killed more than 6,000 settlers. During the Civil War more than 81,000 soldiers died of either typhoid or dysentery. And in the 1890s, the typhoid fever mortality rate in Chicago averaged 65 per 100,000 people a year. The worst year was in 1891, when the typhoid death rate was 174 per 100,000 people.

By all accounts, Mary Mallon worked steadily as a cook from 1900-1906. In the summer of 1906, Mary took a position as a cook for the family of New York banker Charles Henry Warren, who decided to take his family to a rented house on Oyster Bay, Long Island for their summer vacation. On August 24, one of Warren's daughters became violently ill. She was subsequently diagnosed with typhoid fever. Soon, Warren's wife took ill, as well as the gardener and another one of Warren's daughters. Before the summer vacation was over, 6 of the 11 people living in the house were infected with the typhoid bacteria.

George Thompson, who owned the home which Warren had rented, was worried he could no longer rent the house, since he feared the water was contaminated and was the source of the typhoid bacteria. Thompson hired investigators to examine his water and other possible sources of the contamination, but they were unsuccessful in discovering the source of the bacteria.

Thompson then hired George Soper, a civil engineer by trade, who had experience in typhoid fever epidemics. After eliminating one possible cause after another, Soper finally determined that it was the cook, Mary Mallon, three weeks gone from the Warren's employ, who had been the carrier of the disease. But Soper had no definitive proof, so he set out to find Mary and trace her employment history, to see if there was a common denominator in Mary's employment as a cook and typhoid outbreaks.

Through dogged grunt work and numerous knocks on people's

doors, Soper was able to trace Mary's employment record back to 1900. He was not too surprised to discover that from 1900-1907, Mary had worked at seven different households where 22 people had been infected with the typhoid bacteria, including one young girl who had perished from the disease.

It took Soper almost seven months, but in March of 1907, he was able to track down Mary, who was now working as a cook in the family home of Walter Bowen. Soper was intent on getting samples of Mary's urine and blood, but the astounded, befuddled, and belligerent Mary would have none of that.

"I had my first talk with Mary in the kitchen of this house," Soper said. "I was as diplomatic as possible, but I had to say I suspected her of making people sick and that I wanted specimens of her urine, feces, and blood. It did not take Mary long to react to this suggestion. She seized a carving fork and advanced in my direction. I passed rapidly down the long narrow hall, through the tall iron gate, and so to the sidewalk. I felt rather lucky to escape."

Still, Soper was determined and not deterred. The following day, hidden outside the Bowen residence, he waited for Mary to leave the house. When she did, Soper followed Mary (at a safe distance) to her home. Assured Mary was where she could easily be located, Soper left and soon returned with Dr. Bert Raymond Hoobler, who as a doctor might be able to convince Mary that testing her was the right thing to do. This tactic did not work too well either, as Mary cursed at both men and chased them with a knife from her humble abode.

Knowing quite well that Mary would not submit to any testing unless she was forced to do so, Soper went to the New York City Health Department and conferred with the department's commissioner Herman Biggs. Commissioner Biggs agreed with Soper's theories about Mary being a healthy carrier of the typhoid bacteria, and as a result, he decided to send a female doctor, Dr. S. Josephine Baker, to try to reason with Mary. However this tactic didn't work any better than the previous ones. Mary Mallon refused to be tested for the typhoid virus, and she made it very clear to Dr. Baker, that she would not do so without a fight.

Dr. Baker soon returned to Mary's residence, accompanied by five burly policemen and an ambulance.

Dr. Baker described the scene as such: "Mary was on the

lookout for us, and she peered out from the front door, a long kitchen fork in her hand like a rapier. As she lunged at me with the fork, I stepped back, recoiled onto the policeman, and so confused matters that by the time we got through the door, Mary had disappeared. 'Disappeared' is too matter-of-fact a word; she had completely vanished."

Baker and the police searched the house, but alas, there was no Mary Mallon to be found.

Finally, one of the policemen spotted a set of footprints in the corner yard that led from Mary's house to a chair placed up against the fence separating Mary's house from the house next door. The police then spent five hours searching both houses, but to no avail. Finally, one of the policemen spotted "a tiny scrap of blue calico caught in the door of the areaway closet under the high outside stairway leading to the front door."

The policemen forced open the door to the closet, and according to Dr. Baker, "She came out fighting and swearing, both of which she could do with appalling efficiency and vigor. I made another effort to talk to her sensibly and asked her again to let me have the specimens, but it was of no use. By that time she was convinced that the law was wantonly persecuting her, when she had done nothing wrong. She knew she had never had typhoid fever; she was maniacal in her integrity. There was nothing I could do but take her with us. The policemen lifted her into the ambulance, and I literally sat on her all the way to the hospital. It was like being in a cage with an angry lion."

Mary was taken to the Willard Parker Hospital in New York. There, samples were taken and examined, and surprise-surprise, the typhoid bacilli was found in her stool. Without any trial or a hearing of any sort, the Health Department transferred Mary to an isolated cottage, which was part of the Riverside Hospital, on North Brother Island in the East River near the Bronx.

Just like that, Mary Mallon went from being a fine cook, to a pariah, to a prisoner of the state. All without any due process from the courts.

Yet, the New York City health officials said they indeed had the power to detain Mary Mallon indefinitely. The Health Department confirmed their decision by pointing to the powers vested in them from Sections 1169 and 1170 of the Greater New York Charter, which said, "The board of health shall use all reasonable means for ascertaining the existence and cause of disease or peril to life or health, and for averting the same, throughout the city. Said board may remove or cause to be removed to a proper place to be by it designated, any person sick with any contagious, pestilential or infectious disease; shall have exclusive charge and control of the hospitals for the treatment of such cases."

The only problem was, Mary Mallon was not sick with any symptoms of the typhoid virus, and it was not known at the time the statute was written that healthy carriers like Mary even existed. Therefore, the above statute should never have applied to her.

Mary pleaded her case to be released from Riverside Hospital.

"I never had typhoid in my life," she told the press. "And I have always been healthy. Why should I be banished like a leper and compelled to live in solitary confinement with only a dog for a companion?"

In 1907, after Mary had been in confinement for two years, she finally sued the Health Department. For the previous year, Mary had sent her stool samples to a private lab, and they all came back negative. However, when the Health Department did the testing of Mary's stools, 120 of 163 samples came back positive for the typhoid bacteria. So basically, there was a Mexican standoff as to which lab tests were to be believed.

Before she had her day in court, Mary told the press, "This contention that I am a perpetual menace in the spread of typhoid germs is not true. My own doctors say I have no typhoid germs. I am an innocent human being. I have committed no crime and I am treated like an outcast - a criminal. It is unjust, outrageous, uncivilized. It seems incredible that in a Christian community a defenseless woman can be treated in this manner."

Despite Mary's pleas, the presiding judge in the case ruled in the favor of the Health Department, and the person now called "Typhoid Mary" in the press "was remanded to the custody of the Board of Health of the City of New York."

Mary went back to her little isolated cottage on North Brother Island, where her faithful dog greeted her with glee. At this point, Mary was fearful she would spend the rest of her life in that cottage.

In February 1910, in an astounding turn of events, a new Health Commissioner was appointed, and the new commissioner inexplicably ordered Mary to be released immediately. The only stipulation was that Mary had to sign an affidavit stating that she "is prepared to change her occupation (that of a cook), and will give assurance by affidavit that she will upon her release take such hygienic precautions as will protect those with whom she comes in contact from infection."

That being agreed to, Mary was set free after almost four years of confinement.

At this point in time, it would have been a happy ending for everyone if Mary had only stuck to the guidelines in her signed affidavit.

For a while, Mary did menial tasks, like those of a laundress, that did not pay was well as she was paid as a fine cook. It's not clear exactly when, but sometime in 1914, Mary went back to working as a cook. And apparently, her hand-cleaning procedure did not measurably improve.

In January of 1915, the Sloane Maternity Hospital in Manhattan suffered a typhoid fever outbreak. Twenty-five people became ill and two of them died.

Guess who was the newly hired cook for the facility?

Why it was none other than "Typhoid Mary" Mallon herself, working under a fictitious name.

While public opinion was in her favor during Mary's first detention, things were different this time around. Mary, whether she believed it or not, was certified as a healthy carrier of the typhoid bacteria. She knew that was the case, and she defied the Health Department, figuratively ripping up the affidavit she willingly signed. Mary went back to serving contaminated food; food she served to pregnant women. The fact that she used a fictitious name added more weight to Mary's serious transgressions.

Mary Mallon was again shipped off to North Brother Island; to the same cottage she had occupied before (there is no record of her faithful dog being there to greet her this time).

On her second and last visit to North Brother Island (which lasted 23 years until her death), Mary became a "hospital helper," but she was not allowed to touch or even be near any food served to other people. Mary became a minor celebrity, and she was often interviewed by enterprising journalists, whom Mary was not even allowed to offer a glass of water.

In 1932, Mary suffered a severe stroke which left her partially paralyzed and not capable of working in any capacity. At this point, she was transferred from her cottage to a bed in the children's ward of the hospital.

Mary Mallon, more famously known as "Typhoid Mary," died six years later on November 11, 1938. She was 69 years old.

An autopsy found evidence of live typhoid bacteria in Mary's gallbladder.

In a classic case of overkill, the powers in charge at the hospital decided that Mary's body, to destroy all traces of the typhoid bacteria, had to be be cremated immediately.

Mary Mallon's ashes were buried at Saint Raymond's Cemetery in the Bronx.

SNEAK PREVIEW!!

WHITEY BULGER - THE BIGGEST RAT

By - Joe Bruno

Editor – Lawrence Venturato

Published by:

"RATS ARE NOT MADE; PEOPLE ARE BORN RATS."
- Mathew J. Mari, New York City Criminal Attorney for 36 years

Chapter One – "You know who I am. I'm Whitey Bulger."

The first time aspiring musician Joshua Bond met "America's Most Wanted Fugitive," Whitey Bulger, Bond knew the spry 77-year-old retiree as plain old Charlie Gasko.

In 2007, the 26-year-old Bond had just moved to Santa Monica, California with plans of getting involved in the in the Hollywood film business or music business, whichever came first. Bond played guitar in a band called the Kings. Since work was hard to come by, he needed a way to pay the rent and keep food on the table while he pursued his dreams. As a result, Bond took a job as co-manager of the Princess Eugenia Apartments where he received free living quarters in apartment 304, as one of the perks that came with the job. His next-door neighbor, living in apartment 303, was Charlie Gasko and his wife Carol (real name Catherine Greig).

Bond liked to play the guitar in his apartment, sometimes loud enough to be heard clearly through the walls into apartment 303. One day, after playing a particularly stirring riff, Bond heard a knock on his apartment door. This was the first time this phenomenon had occurred, and Bond figured he was about to get a neighborly complaint about the noise. When Bond opened the door, he came face to face with the man he knew as "Charlie" from next door. Bond recoiled, waiting to receive a string of obscenities. Instead, he received a gift.

While Bond stood there quivering, Whitey told Bond he was fond of his music, which was a cross between country western and the blues. That said, Whitey handed Bond a black wool Stetson hat, sporting a leather band sprinkled with silver buttons.

"I don't wear this hat anymore," Whitey told Bond. "I think maybe you could use it."

Bond, tickled pink at the lack of a reprimand, eagerly accepted the hat, and then he bid Whitey goodbye.

But it was not goodbye for long.

Whitey developed the habit of knocking on Bond's door at least twice a week, supposedly to make small talk. The truth is, Bulger, on the run for more than a decade, didn't trust anybody, and he wanted to know all he could about everything connected to the

Princess Eugenia Apartments. To Whitey, being pals with the co-manager was simply good business acumen.

Whitey, being Whitey, found it difficult not to intrude on his young friend without bearing gifts, whether Bond needed them or not. Whitey gave Bond a beard trimmer; a subtle hint maybe Bond was looking a little too scruffy, and Whitey didn't like scruffy.

Whitey was a fitness buff, and he thought Bond was a little out of shape for a man fifty years his junior. So, Whitey dipped into his retirement savings and bought Bond a weight set, complete with a bench and a stomach-crunching thingamajig.

Over the years, Whitey was diligent about taking good care of the assistant manager of the Princess Eugenia Apartments. During the Christmas holidays, instead of cash, Whitey one year bequeathed Bond a spiffy decorative plate, another year he gave Bond an Elvis Presley coffee table (no musician should ever be without one).

However, Whitey was a bit gruff. He insisted on proper decorum when it came to Bond recognizing his benevolence. One holiday season, Whitey left a bag full of Christmas presents at Bond's door. Later, when Whitey and Bonds crossed paths in the underground garage, Bond nary mentioned a word about the gifts. This pissed off Whitey, leading him to reprimand Bond for his lack of respect, even going as far as to "suggest" Bond jot him and Carol a sincere thank-you note. Bond duly complied, kissing off the incident off as nothing more than an old man asking for his due.

During the period from 2007 to 2011, Bond and Whitey maintained a friendly relationship. An uncle/nephew type of rapport developed between the two, where Whitey dispensed advice and Bond made believe he took it. Whitey seemed like a nice elderly man, but Bond was only interested in his music career. Putting up with Whitey was part of the job of being co-manager of the Princess Eugenia Apartments. Bond humored Whitey, and Whitey ate up what seemed to be the young man's deference to Whitey's superior intellect and lifelong experiences.

Bond knew of only one instance where old Charlie Gasko indicated he was capable of violence, and this was because Whitey told Bond about the incident himself.

The Ocean View Manor, a state-licensed residential facility for the mentally disabled, was located a few doors down from Princess Eugenia Apartments. Mentally ill people sometimes do strange things. One resident in particular got his jollies by hiding in the bushes near the facility, and then springing out at an unsuspecting passerby to scare him out of his skin.

One night, as was his wont, Whitey took his moll, Catherine Greig, on a late-night fitness stroll. Suddenly, the eccentric from the Ocean View Manor bounded from the bushes, intending to scare Whitey and Greig.

But Whitey doesn't scare easily.

Whitey told Bond, when the lunatic rushed at him and his wife, Whitey, who always kept a big knife strapped to his ankle, grabbed the man by the neck, pulled out his knife, waved it in the man's face, and said, "If you ever do that to me again, I will cut you to pieces."

Fast-forward to June 22, 2011.

Bond had plans to go to a concert in Hollywood that evening with his pal, Neal Marsh, to see the band, My Morning Jacket. The other co-manager of the Princess Eugenia Apartments, Birgitta Farinelli, had gone on vacation. So, Bond told his assistant, Thea, to substitute for him at the manager's desk, located in the hotel across the street from Princess Eugenia Apartments, while Bond sawed a few afternoon Z's on his apartment couch.

At about 3:30 pm, Bond's phone rang, rousing him from a deep sleep. Thea was on the line and told him F.B.I. agents were in his office. The feds said they needed to speak to Bond immediately about one of the tenants.

This unwelcome intrusion into his afternoon nap did not please Bond. He planned to motor off to Hollywood in a few hours and didn't appreciate any unnecessary distractions.

Thea handed the phone to F.B.I. agent, Scott Garriola, who told Bond that it was imperative that he come to the office immediately, if not sooner.

"Can't this wait until tomorrow?" Bond asked.

"No, it can't," Garriola said. "I need you here now!"

Knowing you don't argue with the feds, Bond dragged himself off his couch, splashed a little water on his face, and then exited his apartment. When he reached the manager's office, Bond met Garriola and another federal agent. The agents showed Bond a string of photos of the couple Bond knew as Charlie and Carol

Gasko. The Feds asked Bond if he could confirm their identities and he did so.

"Yes, I know them," Bond told Garriola. "That's Charlie and Carol from apartment 303."

"Are you absolutely sure?" Garriola asked.

"Definitely; that's them," Bond said.

Garriola told Bond who his neighbors really were, including the information that Whitey was alleged to be a serial murderer. Garriola wanted to arrest Whitey outside his apartment because Whitey's M.O. indicated he kept an arsenal of guns nearby at all times. To facilitate the arrest, Garriola asked Bond if he would be so kind as to go up to apartment 303 and knock on the door.

Bond was not brave. He also was not stupid. Bond didn't mind knocking on apartment 303's door to talk to old Charlie. But confronting a lunatic like Whitey Bulger was not high on Bond's list of things to do.

So, Garriola came up with a plan that would not put Bond in any danger.

Garriola ran down to Whitey's storage locker, located in the garage of the Princess Eugenia Apartments. Using a pair of bolt cutters, Garriola chopped Whitey's lock to pieces, giving the impression petty thieves had stolen Whitey's possessions.

After rushing back to the manager's office, Garriola ordered Bond to phone apartment 303 and tell Whitey his locker had been broken into. By this time, Bond had done a little Googling of Whitey on the office computer. What he saw did not calm his nerves.

Bond later told CBS News, "I went to his (Whitey's) Wikipedia page, and I'm kinda, like, scrolling through, and it's like, murder and extortion, and all this stuff."

Nonetheless, Bond summoned up the courage and phoned apartment 303.

No answer.

Then he tried the cellphone number Carol (Catherine Greig) had given him as a backup.

Still no answer.

Garriola checked with a fellow agent, who confirmed that surveillance definitely showed a man and a woman were present in apartment 303. Garriola tried again to convince Bond to knock on the door of apartment 303.

Bond again refused and who could blame him? He wasn't being paid by the Princess Eugenia Apartments to put his life on the line.

Before Garriola could decide what to do, the phone rang in the manager's office. It was Catherine Greig inquiring if Bond had just called her cell phone. Bond admitted he had, and then told Greig Garriola's malarkey about their storage locker having been broken into.

Grieg hesitated, and then after conferring with Whitey, she said her husband would meet Bond in the garage.

In the underground garage, Whitey didn't get close to his locker. Before he knew what was happening, more than 40 F.B.I. agents in full riot gear, with their guns and rifles pointed his way, surrounded Whitey.

Garriola barked at Whitey, "Get down on your knees!"

Whitey was dressed in white clothes with a white summer hat on his head. (Whitey was a noted Howard Hughes-type neat freak, fearful of the slightest grime.)

"Fuck you!" Whitey said. "There's oil on the floor!"

Garriola told Whitey to move a few steps to his right, and then get down on his knees.

Whitey cursed some more.

Finally, Whitey found a clean spot and got down on his knees, where the agents cuffed Whitey's hands behind his back.

"Please identify yourself," Garriola said.

"I'm Charlie Gasko," Whitey replied.

"You're not Charlie Gasko," Garriola said. "How about we go upstairs and ask your girlfriend to identify you as Charlie Gasko? She's in enough trouble already."

Whitey grunted.

"Okay. You know who I am," Whitey said. "I'm Whitey Bulger."

The 16-year manhunt for the "Most Wanted" criminal in America had finally ended.

If you'd like to grab your copy of "Whitey Bulger – The Biggest Rat," go to:

http://www.amazon.com/dp/B00EZCFVNU

About Joe Bruno:

Mathew J. Mari, New York City criminal lawyer for 40 years, says, "Joe Bruno and I grew up in the same neighborhood on the Lower East Side of New York City. We met and know the most of the same people, some of whom are alleged to be organized crime figures. And I emphasize the word 'alleged.'

"That's why Joe Bruno's insight and style makes it easy for the reader to understand the colorful yet brutal characters that dominated the crime scene in America for two centuries. He knows what he's talking about because he's lived through it.

Joe Bruno's mob books are 'A composite of characters and events, which weaves the denizens of

Joe Bruno's Mobster's books include:

"The Biggest Rat: Whitey Bulger's Decades of Deceit" (September 2013)

"Mobsters, Gangs, Crooks, and Other Creeps - Volume 1 - New York City" (June 2011)

"Mobsters, Gangs, Crooks, and Other Creeps - Volume 2 - New York City" (December 2011)

"Mobsters, Gangs, Crooks, and Other Creeps - Volume 3 - New York City" (March 2012)

"Mobsters, Gangs, Crooks, and Other Creeps - Volume 4" (December 2012)

"Mobsters, Gangs, Crooks, and Other Creeps -Volume 5 – Girlfriends and Wives" (April 2013).

"Murder and Mayhem in the Big Apple - From the Black Hand to Murder Incorporated" (March 2012).

"Mob Wives - Fuhgeddaboudit!" (August 2012)

"Mob Rats – Joe Valachi" (June 2014)

"Mob Rats - Jimmy 'The Weasel' Fratianno (July 2014)

"Mob Rats- Abe 'Kid Twist' Reles" (August 2014)

"Mob Rats – Danny Greene" (September 2014)

"Mob Rats – Bald Jack Rose" (October 2014)

"Mob Molls – Beautiful Broads With Brass Balls – Volume 1" (July 2014)

"Mob Molls – Beautiful Broads With Brass Balls – Volume 2" (November 2014)

"Prohibition Bootleggers and Labor Union Racketeers" (November 2014)

"The Mafia's Greatest Hits – Volume 1" (March 2015)

"Bonnie Parker: Mob Molls - Beautiful Broads with Brass Balls!!" (March 2015)

"Crazy Joe Gallo – The Mafia's Greatest Hits – Volume 2" (August 2015)

"Crazy Joe Gallo: The Screenplay – co-authored with Lawrence Venturato (January 2016)

Boxed sets written by Joe Bruno include:

"Joe Bruno's Mobsters - Three Volume Set" (March 2013)

"Joe Bruno's Mobsters - Six Volume Set" (September 2012).

"Mob Rats – Five Volume Set" (October 2014)
"Mob Molls – Beautiful Broads With Brass Balls – Two Volume Set" (November 2014)

Joe Bruno's fiction books include:
"Snakeheads: Chinese Illegal Immigrant Smugglers - A Screenplay" (June 2013)
"Big Fat Fanny: The Biggest Mafia Killer Ever" (June 2010)

Both fiction books are available in the two-book boxed-set: "Snakeheads: Chinese Illegal Immigrant Smugglers - A Screenplay and Big Fat Fanny: The Biggest Mafia Killer Ever - A Novel" (2013)

What People Are Saying about Joe Bruno's Books:

ANOTHER HISTORY LESSON! – I love Joe Bruno's books. I always say that he's the NYC true crime historian. NYC has had its share of murder and corruption over the past couple of centuries and the author is a wealth of knowledge about it. A must read for any true crime book collector. - RJ Parker - Best Selling Author of True Crime Books

TRUE CRIME AT ITS BEST!! - Joe Bruno has a way of giving real light into his mob stories. His easy writing style pulls you in, and his no BS attitude allows you as a reader to get the full story not just what he chooses to share. There is so much real life history in these books. His books are especially edge of your seat interesting. They are mind blowing, really. I would highly recommend you pick up a copy of one of his books. You'll see what I am talking about. – Brenda Perlin – Adult Contemporary Fiction Author.

INFORMATIVE AND JUST PLAIN GREAT! - I love reading about mobsters and old New York. Joe Bruno is an awesome author. I highly recommend Joe Bruno's books. – Patricia Epps

KNOCK OUT PUNCH! - Joe Bruno delivers a hard punch, well researched, no nonsense book. Fear, hatred, and brutality bring to our awareness in a most convincing and stark manner. The reader is an observer as chills run up and down the spine. Joe Bruno brings full realism to play and bear upon our psyches - Joyce Metzger

WOW WHAT A GREAT BOOK! - I could hardly put it down at night. The way Joe Bruno keeps it short and to the point makes it so easy to read and understand - Dakikle

GREAT READ! - If you are interested in books about gangsters, mobs etc., Joe Bruno is one of the best writers about this subject. You will enjoy all of his books!!!– Rita Moore